INV#139869

BEN FRANKLIN LAUGHING

Ben Franklin Laughing

Anecdotes from
Original Sources
by and about
Benjamin Franklin

Edited with an Introduction by
P.M. ZALL

UNIVERSITY OF CALIFORNIA PRESS
BERKELEY   LOS ANGELES   LONDON

University of California Press
Berkeley and Los Angeles, California

University of California Press, Ltd.
London, England

Library of Congress Cataloging in Publication Data
Main entry under title:

Ben Franklin laughing.

    Includes bibliographical references and indexes.
    1. Franklin, Benjamin, 1706-1790—Anecdotes.
2. Anecdotes—United States.   3. American wit and
humor.   I. Franklin, Benjamin, 1706-1790.   II. Zall,
Paul M.
E302.6.F8B457   818'.102'08   80-19423
ISBN 0-520-04026-0

Printed in the United States of America

1 2 3 4 5 6 7 8 9

For Barnaby and Jan

Contents

Introduction: Anecdotes and Franklin's Fame

The present edition of anecdotes by and about Benjamin Franklin derives from original sources—diaries, memoirs, newspapers, periodicals, scholarly biographies, and popular literature. By nature, anecdotes defy normal standards of originality because they continue to circulate by word of mouth in the public domain even after being recorded for posterity. They often change with each retelling and when written down again appear as something new, or at least reshaped. Thus shaped by succeeding generations, the anecdotes collected here offer a means for measuring the evolution of our attitude toward one of America's favorite founding fathers. This collection is not meant to be exhaustive. To have included multiple versions of each saying or story would have proved tediously repetitious. Instead, the focus is on the kinds rather than the quantity of the anecdotes, with each given in the earliest version to be found. They are presented in order of appearance, and with only a sampling of variants to represent the continual process of change and transformation over 250 years.

Of the two parts of the book, the first includes sixty-six anecdotes from Franklin's correspondence and published writings, excluding such artful pieces as the *Way to Wealth*, the satirical sketches, the longer bagatelles, and the proverbs, since these are easily found elsewhere. What remains might seem surprisingly scanty considering his reputation as a first-rank raconteur with "a prodigious memory for facts and anecdotes,"[1] a memory evident here as he improves on well-known fables (3), adapts earlier anecdotes (16), reapplies current jokes (19), or evokes incidents in his own experience (59). Still, lively as these may be, they ought to be taken only as the written remnants of a multitude of stories celebrated by those who heard Franklin tell them.

The second section of 248 anecdotes from writings by others includes eyewitness reports of sufficient reliability to double the number attributable to Franklin himself. It also includes many others clearly nonsense (237), along with misattributions (156) and garbled recollections, even in anecdotes told about him while he lived (67, 68, 111). It is in this second section that we have a kaleidoscopic view of the way in which generation after generation—from a Finn in the 1750s to a retiring president in the 1950s—has shaped this favorite founding father in its own image.

Of all the anecdotes given here, the largest proportion, about a fifth, focuses on facets of Franklin's personality that we can all share—foibles, follies, and frustrations. In receding order of emphasis, a list of other concerns would include his activities as a patriot, his wit and humor, his homespun ethics, as well as his achievements as a self-made man, politician or diplomat, lover of the ladies, religious being, scientist, confidence man, and activist for sympathetic treatment of red men and blacks. Still, such a list would not reflect the frequency with which each anecdote repeated, only the scale of kinds of concern each reflected.

Even if we could acquire an accurate estimate of the number of times each anecdote reappeared over the years, the figures would doubtless reinforce the theories about the growth of Franklin's fame developed by Richard D. Miles from the latter's reading of nineteenth-century schoolbooks, periodicals, speeches, and sermons.[2] Briefly, Miles found that Franklin's early life in Pennsylvania politics and later life in international diplomacy had made him many powerful enemies. It was they who fabricated the image of him as a shrewd, dissembling, calculating politician whose dominant passion was self-aggrandizement, an image apparent in anecdotes dating from his own time (167). But, Miles points out, theirs was a minority view. In contrast, the more popular view reflected Franklin's own writings, particularly the *Way to Wealth*, with its proverbs on thrift and hard work, and passages from the *Autobiography*, with their inspiring tale of a rise from rags to riches.

The popular view prevailed through the nineteenth century. Miles found that the *Way to Wealth* and the *Autobiography* provided the moral and economic texts for the nation's developing sense of mission through mid-century. Thereafter, the rise of industrialism and the business ethos shifted the stress to his rise to affluence. At the same time, a new xenophobia stressed uniquely American features in his character, and the idolatry of scholars emphasized elements in his personality that made him a universal man, until he became "the most important figure in the writing of American biography between 1860 and 1890."[3]

Those trends Miles described are reflected in the anecdotes printed here. Three events especially stimulated their flow: Franklin's mission to France in 1776 made him the symbol of America abroad. His death in 1790 set off a search for material suited to obituary notices about a figure who had by this time become a national monument and universal man. And then in 1818, William Temple Franklin's edition of his grandfather's *Autobiography* roused surviving friends to recollect anecdotes of their own. As those survivors died off about mid-century, sources of new anecdotes dried up, despite the conscientious efforts of historians and biographers.

Thus in the twentieth century the flow of new anecdotes trickled to droplets, notwithstanding a new storm of charges and countercharges about Franklin's character. In 1917 an eminent Franklinist, Samuel Pennypacker, accused him of "showing ingratitude to friends, usurping others' honors, and securing the favors of women without marriage."[4] Among reputable historians, Max Weber damned him as the watershed of "all that was despicable in both the American character and the capitalist system."[5] And D. H. Lawrence accused him of gross hypocrisy in practicing venery while writing propaganda to repress our instincts. How seriously such charges could be taken may be seen in the refusal of the Daughters of the American Revolution to enroll one Philadelphian because she descended from Franklin.[6]

Reacting to "that tittering denigration, in which our age so frequently asserts its own superiority,"[7] friends of Franklin's fame launched a counterattack that relied less on the old anecdotes or the *Way to Wealth* or the *Autobiography*. Instead they used his less-well-known scatology or salacious sketches. In 1926, Phillips Russell's *Benjamin Franklin the First Civilized American* printed some that had previously circulated in manuscript or in privately printed editions of fifty copies or fewer. In 1929, Bernard Faÿ's *Franklin the Apostle of Modern Times* drew from more than six hundred previously unpublished French documents to demonstrate how Franklin had fooled with the fair ladies of France. Such well-intentioned support contributed little to renew the flow of anecdotes but did energize efforts to prove how human Franklin really was.

In 1932 the eminent bibliophile A. S. W. Rosenbach issued a manifesto in a pamphlet, *All-Embracing Doctor Franklin,* claiming that if his love letters "were as well known as his experiments in electricity or his feats of statesmanship, we would be even prouder of him than we are today . . . as America's upstanding genius" (p. 5). One of those "letters" printed by both Rosenbach and Russell was the then-scandalous "Advice to a Young Man on the Choice of a Mistress" (to the effect that he ought to prefer older to younger women because, among other reasons, they are so grateful). Ten years later that little essay had achieved ultimate respectability with its inclusion in the *Treasury of the World's Great Letters,* a selection of the Book-of-the-Month Club. And fifteen years after that, the whole of Franklin's lusty nature achieved scholarly recognition when A. Owen Aldridge, who had pioneered the study of his anecdotes, wrote a biography, *Benjamin Franklin, Philosopher and Man,* showing how his life and work had been guided by the principle of philoprogenitiveness.

This eagerness to humanize Franklin accelerated in the seventies with the advent of such new historical approaches as psychobiography. In 1973, Richard B. Morris called the first chapter of his *Seven Who Shaped Our Destiny,* "Doctor Franklin: the Senior Citizen as Revolutionary." But his real concern was to analyze the inner conflict between the public and private Franklin—hardworking, frugal, restrained Dr. Franklin versus the lusty Ben with "no scruples about enjoying high living, a liberal sexual code for himself, and bawdy humor" (p. 7). The same conflict fascinated disseminators of popular culture; musicals such as *1776* and the television series by CBS in 1974–1975 exploited the exuberant animal spirits that lay rippling beneath his consummate statecraft. Bruce Bliven summed up the scene in a bicentennial essay for three million subscribers to the *Reader's Digest* in May 1976: "We stress his homely, simple qualities—because that's what we like best in ourselves" (p. 12).

In view of our current curiosity about the lusty aspects of his personality, the anecdotes represented below might seem strangely noncommittal. We do have early instances of his sly repartee with the ladies *(173)*, allusions to the low-class mother of his bastard son *(167)*, even, most shocking of all, rumors of incest with his daughter *(194)*. But these are exceptional. This is not to deny existence of salacious anecdotes about him, only that they are less representative than similar stories he told himself *(54)*.

After all, he created his own image as the great womanizer of the Western world at a time, in his seventies, when he was sometimes so incapacitated by gout, kidney stones, and prostatitis that he could hardly get *out* of bed. His reputation was fabricated in playful love letters composed for Parisiennes with knowledge aforethought that they would circulate in fashionable salons, as delightfully described in Claude-Anne Lopez's *Mon Cher Papa: Franklin and the Ladies of Paris* (1967).[8] For added insurance, he printed some of them on his private press, whence they found their inevitable way to newspapers and popular books *(192)*.

Conversely, many spurious anecdotes derive from his refusing to authorize others to write about him. While he lived and prohibited publication of any biography, newspapers had to print whatever information could be scrounged from rumor, hearsay, or scandal to feed an insatiable public curiosity. Some of this material now sounds like garbled portions of the *Autobiography (93, 94)*, but this can be explained by the fact that the early part of its manuscript, eighty-seven pages, had been surreptitiously copied in the early 1780s and circulated underground until after his death.[9]

Aside from Franklin himself, the most prolific source of new anecdotes was the circle of companions surviving from the Revolutionary era who could refer to diaries or notebooks *(104)* or recollect his conversations *(223)*. When these eyewitnesses passed on, their place was taken by a decidedly different kind of writer whose practice was to fabricate new anecdotes from old ones about other people *(212)*. This practice was traditional among compilers of the jestbooks that flourished in America between the Revolution and the 1840s. So long as they flourished they replenished the stock of anecdotes about Ben Franklin, for he was their favorite single subject.

These jestbooks were more than mere jokebooks, and along with jokes featured anecdotes and historical vignettes of the kind calculated to appeal to the public. Some jestbooks would copy from others verbatim. Many would take the trouble to change names and places. And it is to this latter practice particularly that we are indebted for such cultural monuments as the story about John Hancock appealing to members of the Continental Congress to hang together, and Franklin adding: "Or most assuredly we shall hang separately" *(290)*. One jestbook simply switched names as it lifted that story. In this kind of lively symbiotic relationship, the books fed upon one another and also upon newspapers, almanacs, and periodicals—circulating old anecdotes and stimulating new growth.

After jestbooks faded and after survivors of Franklin's time passed on, it remained for historians and antiquaries to find whatever anecdotes had been so far overlooked. Franklin was, we recall, "the most important figure in the writing of American biography between 1860 and 1890," and yet when James Parton's exhaustive two-volume *Life and Times of Benjamin Franklin* in 1864 printed 130 anecdotes, not one was new. Many new versions of old ones appeared as fillers or "paragraphs" in newspapers, and many more appeared in various collections rewritten in the styles of succeeding generations. But these were merely variations on the same material. That is why the present collection makes no pretense for the period after 1860 at being exhaustive, only representative. For the earlier period, I have tried to include every anecdote about Franklin in the first printed version that I could find.

The anecdotes are arranged by year for each of two sections—those in Franklin's own writings, numbered through 66, and those in writings by others, from 67 on. Each is followed by a concise note about its source. Where no source appears after a particular anecdote, it is one of a series identified in a prefatory note or after the last item in a short series. Many of the notes contain cross-references along with information to help explain allusions, to separate fact from fancy, or to reflect something of the popularity of the anecdote as indicated by reprintings in jestbooks. Some repetition in the notes is intended, on the assumption that the book will be dipped into rather than read consecutively. The three indexes are meant to aid ready reference.

Although working from original texts wherever possible, cited for readers' convenience are the versions of Franklin's own writings as published in the *Papers of Benjamin Franklin* being issued by the Yale University Press, here abbreviated P, followed by volume and page number, thus, P 1:234. Those yet to be printed there may be found in Albert Henry Smyth, ed., *Writings of Benjamin Franklin*, 10 volumes, 1905–1907, cited as "Smyth." And for the *Autobiography*, though working from the manuscript at the Huntington Library, I have cited pertinent page numbers in the *Norton Anthology of American Literature* (1979) Vol. 1, which prints the text prepared by P. M.

Zall and J. A. Leo Lemay for the Norton Critical Edition series. I have used three other means for keeping the notes concise: supplying full names of people in the text itself within brackets; identifying in the notes only those whose connection with Franklin could not be easily found in Appendix B; and using bracketed information in the text to establish certain settings or explain particular events. Such bracketed material, along with ellipses (. . .) therein, are my own unless noted. Otherwise I have tried to retain the original text except for such common abbreviations as *wch* and typographical conventions like the vintage elongated *s*.

Obligations incurred in a project of this kind are incalculable, but I am particularly grateful for permission to use materials at the Huntington Library, from the Readex-Microprint editions of *Early American Imprints* by the American Antiquarian Society, and from reproductions graciously provided by the American Philosophical Society, the Massachusetts Historical Society, and the Pennsylvania Historical Society. Along with the many librarians who patiently answered queries about their holdings, I must also acknowledge the friendly assistance of *Franklin Papers* editors William B. Willcox and Jonathan Dull, Sidney F. Huttner of the Regenstein Library, and my ever-forbearing accomplices, Leo Lemay, Barbara Quinn, and Elisabeth Zall. Without their peculiar advice and counsel, I could have spent another quarter-century seining for still one more anecdote in a stream that must surely seem measureless to man.

NOTES

1. André Morellet, "Anecdotes sur Francklin," *Gazette Nationale*, 15 July 1790, p. 805.

2. "American Image of Franklin," *American Quarterly* 9 (1957): 117–143.

3. Ibid., p. 139.

4. Whitfield J. Bell, Jr., "Benjamin Franklin as an American Hero," *Association of American Colleges Bulletin* 43 (1957): 126.

5. Richard B. Morris, *Seven Who Shaped Our Destiny* (New York, 1973), p. 6.

6. Bell, p. 126.

7. Philip Guadella, *Fathers of the Revolution* (New York, 1926), p. vii.

8. For example, pp. 57, 70, 117–120.

9. P. M. Zall, "The Manuscript and Early Texts of Franklin's *Autobiography*," *HLQ* 39 (1976): 381.

Contents
by Topics

America & Americans

Animals

Aristocrats

Artisans & Workmen

Blacks & Slavery

Books & Booksellers

Children

Constitutional Convention
& Continental Congress

Diplomats & Diplomacy

Doctors & Health

Education

Experiments & Inventions

Extravagance

Fashion & Manners

Foibles & Follies

Founding Fathers

France & the French

Frugality & Generosity

Games & Recreation

Hoaxers & Jokers

Idleness & Industry

Indians

Kings

Lawyers & Lawbreakers

Love & Marriage

Politicians & Generals

Preachers

Printing

Religion

Revolution & Independence

Sailors

Sects

Servants

Visitors

Voltaire & Other Philosophers

Women

Writers & Speakers

PART 1: Anecdotes in Franklin's Own Writings

1 Anecdotes in Franklin's Own Writings

1.   One took the Opportunity of telling us, that in a certain Edition of the Bible, the Printer had, where *David* says *I am fearfully and wonderfully made,* omitted the Letter *(e)* in the last Word, so that it was, *I am fearfully and wonderfully mad;* which occasion'd an ignorant Preacher, who took that Text, to harangue his Audience for half an hour on the Subject of *Spiritual Madness.* Another related to us, that when the Company of Stationers in *England* had the Printing of the Bible in their Hands, the Word *(not)* was left out in the Seventh Commandment, and the whole Edition was printed off with *Thou shalt commit Adultery,* instead of *Thou shalt not,* etc. This material *Erratum* induc'd the Crown to take the Patent from them which is now held by the King's Printer. The *Spectator's* Remark upon this Story is, that he doubts many of our modern Gentlemen have this faulty Edition by 'em, and are not made sensible of the Mistake. A Third Person in the Company acquainted us with an unlucky Fault that went through a whole Impression of Common-Prayer-Books; in the Funeral Service, where these Words are, *We shall all be changed in a moment, in the twinkling of an Eye,* etc. the Printer had omitted the *(c)* in *changed,* and it read thus, *We shall all be hanged,* etc.

> In a discussion about printers' errors, the *Pennsylvania Gazette*, 13 March 1730 (P 1:169–170). The *Spectator* for 11 August 1714, said: "I am afraid that very many young Profligates, of both Sexes

... observe the Commandment according to that faulty Read-
ing" (ed. D. F. Bond, 5 vols. [1965], 4:580). For variants of the
"We shall all be hanged" story, see 90, and the Preface to *Poor
Richard's Almanac*, 1750 (*P* 3:438).

2.   A certain Curate lived in the Island of *Jamaica*, who loved
his Bottle, no Curate better; he chanced to be drinking in a Tavern,
when he was called upon to do the last Offices to a Brother departed;
upon which with great Reluctance he leaves his Company, but told
them he would return immediately; away he hies to the Place of Burial,
and, as is usual, reads over the Service for the Dead, till he came to
the Words, *I heard a Voice from Heaven, saying, blessed*, etc. at which
he was interrupted by one of his Companions, who had followed
him from the Ale house, with a *"By G——— that's a D———'d Lye; for
I have been drinking with you all Day at Mother ———'s, and if you had
heard that Voice, I could have heard it too, for my Ears are as good as yours."*

In the *Pennsylvania Gazette*, 23 April 1730, commenting on
haunted houses and a poltergeist that appears only to certain
persons.

3.   I take leave to conclude with an old Fable, which some
of my Readers have heard before, and some have not.
          "A certain well-meaning Man and his Son, were travelling
towards a Market Town, with an Ass which they had to sell. The
Road was bad; and the old Man therefore rid, but the Son went
a-foot. The first Passenger they met, asked the Father if he was not
ashamed to ride by himself, and suffer the poor Lad to wade along
thro' the Mire; this induced him to take up his Son behind him: He
had not travelled far, when he met others, who said, they were two
unmerciful Lubbers to get both on the Back of that poor Ass, in such
a deep Road. Upon this the old Man gets off, and let his Son ride
alone. The next they met called the Lad a graceless, rascally young
Jackanapes, to ride in that Manner thro' the Dirt, while his aged
Father trudged along on Foot; and they said the old Man was a Fool,
for suffering it. He then bid his Son come down, and walk with him,
and they travell'd on leading the Ass by the Halter; 'till they met
another Company, who called them a Couple of senseless Blockheads,
for going both on Foot in such a dirty Way, when they had an empty
Ass with them, which they might ride upon. The old Man could bear

no longer; My Son, said he, it grieves me much that we cannot please all these People: Let us throw the Ass over the next bridge, and be no farther troubled with him."

> In the *Pennsylvania Gazette* for 3 June–10 June 1731, concluding an editorial on the printer's right to publish without regard to public opinion (P 1:199). The fable was Fable 52 in the standard collection by Roger l'Estrange, *Fables of Aesop, and Other Mythologists* (1692), but BF's lively, colloquial version is a fresh retelling.

4.   Honest Men often go to Law for their Right; when Wise Men would sit down with the Wrong, supposing the first Loss least. In some Countries the Course of the Courts is so tedious, and the Expence so high, that the Remedy, *Justice*, is worse than, *Injustice*, the Disease. In my Travels I once saw a Sign call'd *The Two Men at Law*; One of them was painted on one Side, in a melancholy Posture, all in Rags, with this Scroll, *I have lost my Cause*. The other was drawn capering for Joy, on the other Side, with these Words, *I have gain'd my Suit*; but he was stark naked.

> In *Poor Richard's Almanac* for 1742, headed "Courts" (P 2:339).

5.   I remember a notable Woman, who was fully sensible of the intrinsic Value of *Time*. Her Husband was a Shoemaker, and an excellent Craftsman, but never minded how the Minutes passed. In vain did she inculcate to him, That *Time is Money*. He had too much Wit to apprehend her, and it prov'd his Ruin. When at the Alehouse among his idle Companions, if one remark'd that the Clock struck Eleven, *What is that*, says he, *among us all?* If she sent him Word by the Boy, that it had struck Twelve; *Tell her to be easy, it can never be more*. If, that it had struck One, *Bid her be comforted, for it can never be less*.

> In *Poor Richard's Almanac* for 1751, under "January," illustrating the point that "Lost Time is never found again" (P 4:86–87).

6.   The Tatler tells us of a Girl who was observ'd to grow suddenly proud, and none could guess the Reason, till it came to be known that she had got on a pair of new Silk Garters. . . . I fear I have not so much Reason to be proud as the Girl had; for a Feather

in the Cap is not so useful a Thing, or so serviceable to the Wearer, as a Pair of good Silk Garters.

> In a letter to Jared Eliot of Connecticut, a Congregational preacher, physician, and scientist, 12 April 1753, about the king of France's compliments for BF's electrical discoveries (*P* 4:466–467).
>
> The *Tatler*, no. 151, 28 March 1710, has the girl wearing "striped," rather than silk, garters.

7.   We had here some years since a Transylvanian Tartar, who had travelled much in the East, and came hither merely to see the West, intending to go home thro' the Spanish West Indies, China, etc. He asked me one day what I thought might be the Reason that so many and such numerous nations, as the Tartars in Europe and Asia, the Indians in America, and the Negroes in Africa, continued a wandring careless Life, and refused to live in Cities, and to cultivate the arts they saw practiced by the civilized part of Mankind. While I was considering what answers to make him; I'll tell you, says he in his broken English, God make man for Paradise, he make him for to live lazy; man make God angry, God turn him out of Paradise, and bid him work; man no love work; he want to go to Paradise again, he want to live lazy; so all mankind love lazy.

> In a letter to Peter Collinson, his London agent and fellow scientist, 9 May 1753, about assimilating German immigrants and the relativity of cultures (*P* 4:480–481). The "Tartar" is identified as Samuel Domien, a Greek Orthodox priest who visited BF in 1748.

8.   The little value Indians set on what we prize so highly under the name Learning appears from a pleasant passage that happened some years since at a Treaty between one of our Colonies and the Six Nations; when every thing had been settled to the Satisfaction of both sides, and nothing remained but a mutual exchange of civilities, the English Commissioners told the Indians, they had in their Country a College for the instruction of Youth who were there taught various languages, Arts, and Sciences; that there was a particular foundation in favour of the Indians to defray the expense of the Education of any of their sons who should desire to take the Benefit of it. And now if the Indians would accept of the Offer, the

English would take half a dozen of their brightest lads, and bring them up in the Best manner; The Indians after consulting on the proposal replied that it was remembered some of their Youths had formerly been educated in that College, but it had been observed that for a long time after they returned to their Friends, they were absolutely good for nothing being neither acquainted with the true methods of killing deer, catching Beaver or surprising an enemy. The Proposition however, they looked on as a mark of the kindness and good will of the English to the Indian Nations which merited a grateful return; and therefore if the English Gentlemen would send a dozen or two of their Children to Onondago the great Council would take care of their Education, bring them up in really what was the best manner and make men of them.

> In the same letter as 6 (P 4:482–483). The actual treaty was concluded on 4 July 1744, when the Indian response was more polite: "We thank you for your Invitation; but our Customs differing from yours, you will be so good as to excuse us" (Carl Van Doren and Julian P. Boyd, ed., *Indian Treaties Printed by BF* [1938], p. 76). For variant, see *41*.

9.   As to our lodging, 'tis on deal feather beds, in warm blankets, and much more comfortable than when we lodged at our inn, the first night after we left home, for the woman being about to put very damp sheets on the bed we desired her to air them first; half an hour afterwards, she told us the bed was ready, and the sheets *well aired*. I got into bed, but jumped out immediately, finding them as cold as death, and partly frozen. She had *aired* them indeed, but it was out upon the *hedge*.

> In a letter to his wife, 25 January 1756, referring to the trip from Philadelphia to Bethlehem in mid-December 1755, on his way to the frontier, where this letter was written (P 6:365).

10.   This Prudence of not attempting to give Reasons before one is sure of Facts, I learnt from one of your Sex, who, as [John] Selden tells us, being in company with some Gentlemen that were viewing and considering something which they call'd a Chinese Shoe, and disputing earnestly about the manner of wearing it, and how it could possibly be put on; put in her Word, and said modestly, *Gentlemen, are you sure it is a Shoe? Should not that be settled first?*

In a letter of 13 September 1760 to Mary Stevenson, daughter
of his London landlady, who had asked why water warms when
pumped (*P* 9:212–213). BF changed the anecdote as it appeared
in John Selden's *Table Talk* (1689), p. 50: "the Reason of a
Thing is not to be enquired after, till you are sure the Thing it
self be so. . . . 'Twas an excellent Question of my Lady *Cotten*,
when Sir *Robert Cotten* was magnifying of a Shooe, which was
Moses's or *Noah's*, and wondring at the strange Shape and
Fashion of it: *But Mr.* Cotten, says she, are you sure it is a Shooe"
(Edward Arber, ed. [1868], pp. 100–101).

11.   Let me give you a pleasant Instance of the Prejudice some
have entertained against your Work [in typography]. Soon after I
returned, discoursing with a Gentleman concerning the Artists of
Birmingham, he said you would be a Means of blinding all the Readers
in the Nation, for the Strokes of your Letters being too thin and
narrow, hurt the Eye, and he could never read a Line of them without
Pain. I thought, said I, you were going to complain of the Gloss on
the Paper, some object to: No, no, says he, I have heard that mentioned, but it is not that; 'tis in the Form and Cut of the Letters
themselves; they have not that natural and easy Proportion between
the Height and Thickness of the Stroke, which makes the common
Printing so much more comfortable to the Eye. You see this Gentleman was a Connoisseur. In vain I endeavoured to support your *Character* against the Charge; he knew what he felt, he could see the
Reason of it, and several other Gentlemen among his Friends had
made the same Observation, etc. Yesterday he called to visit me,
when, mischievously bent to try his Judgment, I stept into my Closet,
tore off the Top of Mr. [William] Caslon's Specimen [of type], and
produced it to him as yours brought with me from Birmingham, saying, I had been examining it since he spoke to me, and could not
for my Life perceive the Disproportion he mentioned, desiring him
to point it out to me. He readily undertook it, and went over the
several Founts, shewing me every-where what he thought Instances
of that Disproportion; and declared, that he could not then read the
Specimen without feeling very strongly the Pain he had mentioned
to me. I spared him that Time the Confusion of being told, that these
were the Types he had been reading all his Life with so much Ease
to his Eyes; the Types his adored Newton is printed with, on which
he has pored not a little; nay, the very Types his own Book is printed

with, for he is himself an Author; and yet never discovered this painful Disproportion in them, till he thought they were yours.

> In a letter to the Birmingham (England) typographer John Baskerville, who published it as a testimonial in the London papers, August 1763, though it was probably written a year or two earlier (P 9:259–260).

12.   Judges in their Decisions often use Precedents. I have somewhere met with one that is what the Lawyers call *a Case in Point.* The Church People and the Puritans in a Country Town, had once a bitter Contention concerning the Erecting of a Maypole, which the former desir'd and the latter oppos'd. Each Party endeavour'd to strengthen itself by obtaining the Authority of the Mayor, directing or forbidding a Maypole. He heard their Altercation with great Patience, and then gravely determin'd thus; You that are for having no Maypole shall have no Maypole; and you that are for having a Maypole shall have a Maypole. Get about your Business and let me hear no more of this Quarrel. So methinks Lord Mareschal might say; You that are for no more Damnation than is proportion'd to your Offences, have my Consent that it may be so: And you that are for being damn'd eternally, G—d eternally d——n you all, and let me hear no more of your Disputes.

> In a letter to his friend, the philosopher and historian David Hume, 19 May 1762, talking about George Keith, Earl Marischal, governor of Neuchâtel, asked to settle a dispute over dismissing a pastor for not preaching on eternal damnation (P 10:83). In a later London jestbook, *Festival of Wit* (1783), the king of Prussia in the same predicament echoes the concluding sentence: "Since my subjects of Neuf Chatel are so fond of ever-lasting damnation, they have my free leave to be damned to all eternity" (p. 6).

13.   While the *Moors* governed [Spain], and the *Spaniards* were mixed with them, a *Spanish* Cavalier, in a sudden Quarrel, slew a young *Moorish* Gentleman, and fled. His Pursuers soon lost Sight of him, for he had, unperceived, thrown himself over a Garden Wall. The Owner, a *Moor*, happening to be in his Garden, was addressed by the *Spaniard* on his Knees, who acquainted him with his Case, and implored Concealment. *Eat this,* said the *Moor,* giving him Half

a Peach; *you now know that you may confide in my Protection.* He then
locked him up in his Garden Apartment, telling him, that as soon as
it was Night he would provide for his Escape to a Place of more
Safety.— The *Moor* then went into his House, where he had scarce
seated himself, when a great Croud, with loud Lamentations, came to
his Gate, bringing the Corps of his Son, that had just been killed by
a *Spaniard.* When the first Shock of Surprize was a little over, he
learnt, from the Description given, that the fatal Deed was done by
the Person then in his Power. He mentioned this to no One; but as
soon as it was dark, retired to his Garden Apartment, as if to grieve
alone, giving Orders that none should follow him. There accosting
the *Spaniard,* he said, *Christian, the Person you have killed, is my Son:
His Body is now in my House. You ought to suffer; but you have eaten
with me, and I have given you my Faith, which must not be broken. Follow
me.*— He then led the astonished *Spaniard* to his Stables, mounted
him on one of his fleetest Horses, and said, *Fly far while the Night
can cover you. You will be safe in the Morning. You are indeed guilty of
my Son's Blood, but God is just and good, and I thank him that I am innocent of yours, and that my Faith given is preserved.*

> In BF's pamphlet, *Narrative of the Late Massacres in Lancaster
> County* (1764), pp. 18–19, contrasting this instance of hospitality
> to the behavior of the Paxton Boys, who had massacred Indians
> in protective custody at Conestoga Manor (P 11:18–19).

14.   Will it be permitted me to adduce on this Occasion, an
Instance of the like Honour in a poor unenlightened *African Negroe.*
I find it in Capt. *Seagrave's* Account of his Voyage to *Guinea.* He
relates that a *New-England* Sloop, trading there in 1752, left their
second Mate, *William Murray,* sick on Shore, and sailed without him.
Murray was at the House of a Black, named *Cudjoe,* with whom he
had contracted an Acquaintance during their Trade. He recovered,
and the Sloop being gone, he continued with his black Friend, till
some other Opportunity should offer of his getting home. In the mean
while, a *Dutch* Ship came into the Road, and some of the Blacks
going on board her, were treacherously seized, and carried off as
Slaves. Their Relations and Friends, transported with sudden Rage,
ran to the House of *Cudjoe* to take Revenge, by killing *Murray. Cudjoe*
stopt them at the Door, and demanded what they wanted? The White
Men, said they, have carried away our Brothers and Sons, and we
will kill all White Men;— give us the White Man that you keep in

your House, for we will kill him. *Nay*, said *Cudjoe; the White Men that carried away your Brothers are bad Men, kill them when you can catch them; but this White Man is a good Man, and you must not kill him.*— But he is a White Man, they cried; the White Men are all bad; we will kill them all.— *Nay*, says he, *you must not kill a Man, that has done no Harm, only for being white. This Man is my Friend, my House is his Fort, and I am his Soldier. I must fight for him. You must kill me, before you can kill him.*— *What good Man will ever come again under my Roof, if I let my Floor be stained with a good Man's Blood!*— The *Negroes* seeing his Resolution, and being convinced by his Discourse that they were wrong, went away ashamed. In a few days *Murray* ventured abroad again with *Cudjoe*, when several of them took him by the Hand, and told him they were glad they had not killed him; for as he was good (meaning an innocent) Man, *their God would have been angry, and would have spoiled their Fishing.*

> From the same pamphlet as *13*, pp. 21–22. I have not found "Captain Seagrave's Account of his Voyage to Guinea" nor the source of the story in *13*. BF's pamphlet was reprinted in the *Gentleman's Magazine* for April 1764 (34:173–178), and *14* was picked up in Abbé Raynal's *History of the Three Indies* (1770) as a "well-authenticated fact" (6 vols. [Edinburgh, 1804], 4:80–81).

15.   Two journeymen *Snips*, during the season of little business, agreed to make a trip to *Paris*, with each a fine lac'd waistcoat, in which they promised themselves the great pleasure of being received and treated as *gentlemen*. On the road from *Calais* at every inn, when they called for any thing hastily, they were answered, *Tout à l'heure, Tout à l'heure*; which not a little surprized them. At length, D——— these French scoundrels, says one, how *shrewd* they are! I find it won't do;—e'en let us go back again to London.— Aye, says t'other, they must certainly deal with the devil, or dress'd as we are dress'd, they could not possibly all at first sight have known us to be *two taylors.*

> In a letter to the London *Gazetteer and New Daily Advertiser*, 14 January 1766, replying to a writer who claimed Americans could not distinguish gentlemen from scoundrels (P 13:38–39), reprinted in the *Pennsylvania Chronicle* for 2 March–9 March 1767.

16.   [The Government intended to force Americans to pay for the stamps printed but not used now that the Stamp Act had been

repealed.] The whole Proceeding would put one in Mind of the Frenchman that used to accost English and other Strangers on the Pont-Neuf* [*Note:* A Bridge over the River Seine, leading to Paris], with many Compliments, and a red hot Iron in his Hand; *Pray; Monsieur Anglois,* says he, *Do me the Favour to let me have the Honour of thrusting this hot Iron into your Backside?* Zoons, what does the Fellow mean! Begone with your Iron, or I'll break your Head! *Nay, Monsieur,* replies he, *if you do not chuse it, I do not insist upon it. But at least, you will in Justice have the Goodness to pay me something for the Heating of my Iron.*

> Among the most widely reprinted of BF's anecdotes, this prob-
> ably appeared in a London newspaper of early 1766, but here
> derives from the *Pennsylvania Chronicle* for 23 March 1767 (P
> 13:184). A variant of 1788 (77), elicited his sister's complaint
> about the variant's profanity; see 56. My friend J. A. Leo Lemay
> pointed out to me BF's probable source in the "Dedication" to
> Robert Hunter's *Androboros* (1714), which talks about "an Odd
> Fellow upon *Pont* Neuf" who got his livelihood this way, accost-
> ing "Gentlemen who pass'd that way, with this Complement,
> *Good Sir! Pray Sir! give me leave to run my hot Iron into your Arse,"*
> and when they refused, asking them to at least pay "for the heat-
> ing of my Iron, and there is no harm done" (p. iii; rpt., *Bulletin
> of the New York Public Library,* 68 [1964]: 153–190).

17.   *Konnedohago,* the young Warrior, took up the discourse, and said, You tell us that the great Manitta made all things in the first six days. I find we know some things that you do not know. Your book does not tell you every thing. At least if your Manitta made all the things of your country in the first six days, it was not so in this Indian country; for some things were not made till many generations after, and they were made by our Manitta's Daughter. I will tell you, says he, how it happened, as I learnt it when I last hunted among the *Oneidas.* Nine *Oneida* Warriors passing near a certain hill, not far from the head of the *Susquehannah,* saw a most beautiful young Woman descend naked from the clouds, and seat herself on the ground upon that hill. Then they said, this is the great Manitta's Daughter, let us go to her, welcome her into our country, and present her some of our venison. They gave her a fawn's tongue broiled, which she eat, and thanking them, said, come to this place again after twelve moons, and you will find, where I now sit, some things

that you have never yet seen, and that will do you good. So saying she put her hands on the ground, arose, went up into the cloud, and left them. They came accordingly after twelve moons, and found growing, where she had pressed the ground with her right hand, corn, where with her left hand, beans; and where her back parts had pressed it, there grew tobacco. At this origin of tobacco, all the young Indians laughed; but old *Canassatego*, reproving them and the teller of the story, said, you are a young man, or you would not have told before this white man such a story. It is a foolish *Oneida* tale. If you tell him such tales, what can you expect but to make him laugh at our Indian stories as much as you sometimes do at his?

> In the London *Chronicle*, 28 June 1768, as a pretended excerpt from a nonexistent book, *The Captivity of William Henry (P* 15: 151–152). This hoax was identified by A. Owen Aldridge, "Franklin's Deistical Indians," PAPS 94 (1950): 398–410. For a variant of 1783, see *42*.

18.   The situation of the colonies seems similar to that of the cows in the fable; forbidden to suckle their own calves, and daily drawn dry, yet they parted with their milk willingly; but when moreover a tax came to be demanded of them, and that too to be paid *in grass* of which they had already too short a provision; it was no wonder they thought their masters unreasonable, and resolved for the future to suck one another.

> In the *Pennsylvania Chronicle*, 12 December 1768 (*P* 15:66–67). This fable was included with two others in the London *Public Advertiser*, 2 January 1770 (see *20, 21*), where it read: "A Herd of Cows had long afforded Plenty of Milk, Butter, and Cheese to an avaricious Farmer, who grudged them the Grass they subsisted on, and at length mowed it to make Money of the Hay, leaving them to *shift for Food* as they could, and yet still expected to milk *them* as before; but the Cows, offended with his Unreasonableness, resolved for the future *to suckle one another*" (*P* 17:3).

19.   Mr. [George] Grenville speaking of the Inefficiency of the present Ministry, compar'd them to two raw Sailors who were got up into the round Top, and understanding nothing of the Business, pretended however to be very busy. *What are you doing there, Jack,*

says the Boatswain. *Nothing*, says Jack. *And pray what are you about, Tom? I*, says Tom, *am helping him.*

> In a letter to his political ally in Philadelphia, Joseph Galloway, 7 February 1769, reporting on parliamentary debates about American affairs (P 16:40). Grenville, as first lord of the treasury, had been responsible for the Stamp Act. The London jestbook, *Treasury of Wit* (2 vols., 1786), says this joke used to be applied to "the present Ministry" by the comedian James Quin (2:146).

20.   An Eagle, King of Birds, sailing on his Wings aloft over a Farmer's Yard, saw a Cat there basking in the Sun, *mistook it for a Rabbit*, stoop'd, seized it, and carried it up into the Air, *intending to prey on it*. The Cat turning, set her Claws into the Eagle's Breast; who, finding his Mistake, opened his Talons, and would have let her drop; but Puss, unwilling to fall so far, held faster; and the Eagle, to get rid of the Inconvenience, found it necessary to *set her down where he took her up*.

21.   A Lion's Whelp was put on board a Guinea Ship bound to America as a Present to a Friend in that Country: It was tame and harmless as a Kitten, and therefore not confined, but suffered to walk about the Ship at Pleasure. A stately, full-grown English Mastiff, belonging to the Captain, despising the Weakness of the young Lion, frequently took it's *Food* by Force, and often turned it out of it's Lodging Box, when he had a Mind to repose therein himself. The young Lion nevertheless grew daily in Size and Strength, and the Voyage being long, he became at last a more equal Match for the Mastiff; who continuing his Insults, received a stunning blow from the Lion's Paw that fetched his Skin over his Ears, and deterred him from any future Contest with such growing Strength; regretting that he had not rather secured it's Friendship than provok'd it's Enmity.

> Along with the variant, *18*, both fables were included in the London *Public Advertiser*, 2 January 1770 as "New Fables, humbly inscribed to the S[ecretary] of Sta[t]e for the American Department" (P 17:3–4). For John Adams's story of how *20* was composed, see the variant, *148*.

22.   There is a Story of two little Boys in the Street; one was crying bitterly; the other came to him to ask what was the Matter?

I have been, says he, for a pennyworth of Vinegar, and I have broke the Glass and spilt the Vinegar, and my Mother will whip me. *No, she won't whip you* says the other. Indeed she will, says he. *What*, says the other, *have you then got ne'er a Grandmother?*

> In a letter to his wife, 3 October 1770, teasing her about spoiling their baby grandson (P 17:239).

23.   I believe I have omitted mentioning that in my first Voyage from Boston, being becalm'd off Block Island, our People set about catching Cod and hawl'd up a great many. Hitherto I had stuck to my Resolution of not eating animal Food; and on this Occasion, I consider'd with my Master Tryon, the taking every Fish as a kind of unprovok'd Murder, since none of them had or ever could do us any Injury that might justify the Slaughter. All this seem'd very reasonable. But I had formerly been a great Lover of Fish, and when this came hot out of the Frying Pan, it smelt admirably well. I balanc'd some time between Principle and Inclination: till I recollected, that when the Fish was opened, I saw smaller Fish taken out of their Stomachs: Then, thought I, if you eat one another, I don't see why we mayn't eat you. So I din'd upon Cod very heartily and continu'd to eat with other People, returning only now and then occasionally to a vegetable Diet. So convenient a thing it is to be a *reasonable Creature*, since it enables one to find or make a Reason for every thing one has a mind to do.

> In the *Autobiography*, NCE pp. 314–315. "Master Tryon" refers to Thomas Tryon, who wrote a series of self-help medical books promoting the virtues of a vegetarian diet, most notably *The Way to Health, Wealth and Happiness* (1682–1698).

24.   Charles I ordered his Proclamation authorizing Sports on a Sunday, to be read in all Churches. Many Clergymen comply'd, some refus'd and others hurry'd through as indistinctly as possible. But one, whose Congregation expected no such thing from him, did nevertheless, to their great Surprize, read it distinctly. He follow'd it, however, with the Fourth Commandment, *Remember to keep holy the Sabbath Day*, and then said, Brethren, I have laid before you the Command of your King and the Commandment of your God. I leave it to your selves to judge which of the two ought rather to be observed.

In a letter to Samuel Cooper, Boston clergyman and patriot, whose later correspondence kept BF informed of events in America during the War, 13 January 1772 (P 19:15–16). BF's story derived ultimately from *The Earl of Strafforde's Letters*, ed. William Knowler (2 vols., 1739), reporting that sports were to be allowed after evening services rather than on Sunday, as BF has it, and the preacher read all ten commandments (1:166).

25.   'Tis a most wicked Distemper, and often puts me in mind of the Saying of a Scotch Divine to some of his Brethren who were complaining that their Flocks had of late been infected with *Arianism* and *Socinianism*. Mine, says he, is infected with a worse *ism* than either of those. Pray, Brother, what can that be? It is, the Rheuma*tism*!

In a letter to Anthony Tissington, who had earlier been his host, 28 January 1772 (P 19:46). Mrs. Tissington had been suffering rheumatic pains.

26.   At the opening of one of the bottles [of Madeira], at the house of a friend where I then was, three drowned flies fell into the first glass that was filled. Having heard it remarked that drowned flies were capable of being revived by the rays of the sun, I proposed making the experiment upon these; they were therefore exposed to the sun upon a sieve, which had been employed to strain them out of the wine. In less than three hours, two of them began by degrees to recover life. They commenced by compulsive motions of the thighs, and at length they raised themselves upon their legs wiped their eyes with their fore feet, beat and brushed their wings with their hind feet, and soon after began to fly, finding themselves in Old England, without knowing how they came thither. The third continued lifeless till sunset, when, losing all hopes of him, he was thrown away.

In a letter to the editor of his works in French, Jacques Barbeu-Dubourg, about the end of April 1773, included in *OEuvres de M. Franklin* (1773), 1:328 (P 20:190; trans. Smyth 6:43). For a variant, see 258.

27.   I begin to be a little of the Sailors Mind when they were handing a Cable out of a Store into a Ship, and one of 'em said, 'Tis a long heavy Cable, I wish we could see the End of it. D——n me, says another, if I believe it has any End: Somebody has cut it off.

> In a letter to his Pennsylvania ally, Joseph Galloway, 6 April
> 1773, on progress in trying to establish a new colony in what is
> now West Virginia (P 20:150).

28.   Cotton [Mather] I remember in the Vigour of his Preaching and Usefulness. And particularly in the Year 1723, now half a Century since, I had Reason to remember, as I still do a Piece of Advice he gave me. I had been some time with him in his Study, where he condescended to entertain me, a very Youth, with some pleasant and instructive Conversation. As I was taking my Leave he accompany'd me thro' a narrow Passage at which I did not enter, and which had a Beam across it lower than my Head. He continued Talking which occasion'd me to keep my Face partly towards him as I retired, when he suddenly cry'd out, Stoop! Stoop! Not immediately understanding what he meant, I hit my Head hard against the Beam. He then added, *Let this be a Caution to you not always to hold your Head so high; Stoop, young Man, stoop—as you go through the World—and you'll miss many hard Thumps.* This was a way of hammering Instruction into one's Head: And it was so far effectual, that I have ever since remember'd it, tho' I have not always been able to practise it.

> In a letter to Samuel Mather, son of Cotton Mather, 7 July
> 1773, thanking him for two essays and sending him another
> about religious toleration in return (P 20:287). The anecdote
> remained a favorite in jestbooks; for example, *Comical Jester*
> (1810), p. 10.

29.   What made ["An Edict of the King of Prussia"] the more noticed here was, that people in reading it, were, as the phrase is, *taken in,* till they had got half through it, and imagined it a real edict, to which mistake I suppose the king of Prussia's *character* must have contributed. [The real king of Prussia had recently issued an edict claiming parts of what is now Holland.] I was down at lord Le Despencer's when the post brought that day's papers. Mr. Whitehead was there too [Paul Whitehead, the author of Manners (a satiric poem)] who runs early through all the papers, and tells the company what he finds remarkable. He had them in another room, and we were chatting in the breakfast parlour, when he came running in to us, out of breath, with the paper in his hand. Here! says he, here's news for ye! *Here's the king of Prussia, claiming a right to this kingdom!* All stared, and

I as much as any body; and he went on to read it. When he had read two or three paragraphs, a gentleman present said, *Damn his impudence, I dare say, we shall hear by next post that he is upon his march with one hundred thousand men to back this.* Whitehead, who is very shrewd, soon after began to smoke it, and looking in my face said, *I'll be hanged if this is not some of your American jokes upon us.* The reading went on, and ended with abundance of laughing, and a general verdict that it was a fair hit: and the piece was cut out of the paper and preserved in my lord's collection.

> In a letter to his son William, governor of New Jersey, 6 October 1773 (P 20:438–439). BF's hoaxing "Edict" had appeared in the London *Public Advertiser* for 22 September.

30.   This puts one in mind of the Chimney-sweeper condemn'd to be hang'd for Theft, who being charitably visited by a good Clergyman for whom he had work'd, said, *I hope your Honour will take my Part, and get a Reprieve for me, and not let my Enemies have their Will; because it is upon your Account that they have prosecuted and sworn against me.* On my Account! How can that be? *Why, Sir, because as how, ever since they knew I was employ'd by your Honour, they resolv'd upon my Ruin; for they are Enemies to all Religion; and they hate you and me and every body in black.*

> In a reply to a writer in the London *Public Advertiser* of 29–30 October 1773, who had maintained anyone that was his enemy was therefore an enemy of the king. BF apparently did not send this reply, though he had made two copies of the manuscript (P 20:455).

31.   I suppose Mrs. Brownrigg did not succeed in making the Parmesan Cheese, since we have heard nothing of it. But as a Philosophess, she will not be discouraged by one or two Failures. Perhaps some Circumstance is omitted in the Receipt, which by a little more Experience she may discover. The foreign Gentleman, who had learnt in England to like boiled Plumbpudding, and carried home a Receipt for making it, wondered to see it brought to his Table in the Form of a Soup. The Cook declar'd he had exactly followed the Receipt. And when that came to be examined, a small, but important Circumstance appeared to have been omitted. There was no Mention of the Bag.

In a letter to William Brownrigg, a Lake Country physician who had been his host the previous year, 7 November 1773 (P 20:464).

32. There once was an Officer, a man of means, named Montresor, who grew very ill. His Curate, believing he was about to die, advised him to make his Peace with God, to be received in Paradise. I have little worry on that Score, says Montresor; for last night I had a Vision that left me completely at ease. What Vision did you have? says the good Priest. I was, says he, at the Gate of Paradise, with a Crowd of People who wished to enter. And St. Peter asked each one what his Religion was. One replied, I am a Roman Catholic. Is that so? said St. Peter; Come in, and take your Place there among the Catholics. Another says he was of the Anglican Church. Is that so? says St. Peter, come in, and place yourself among the Anglicans. Another says that he was a Quaker. Come in, says St. Peter, and take a Place among the Quakers. At last he asked me my Religion. Alas, I reply, unfortunately poor Jaques Montresor has hardly any. That's too bad, says the Saint—I don't know where to put you; but come in anyway, and place yourself wherever you can.

> Entitled "Conte," printed by BF at his press in Passy in French, here translated from the facsimile in L. S. Livingston, F & His Press at Passy (1914), p. 42. Reprints, very popular in France, are discussed in A. O. Aldridge, F & His French Contemporaries (1957), pp. 172–174.

33. A Beggar asked a rich Bishop for Charity, demanding a pound.—"A Pound to a beggar! That would be extravagant."— "A Shilling then!"— "Oh, it's still too much!"— "A twopence then or your Benediction."— "Of course, I will give you my Benediction."— "I don't want it, for if it were worth a twopence, you wouldn't give it me."

> In an undated letter to his Parisienne friend, Mme. Brillon, teasing about her amorous restraint (Smyth 10:423; trans. Bernard Fay in BF, Apostle of Modern Times [1929], p. 466).

34. You desired, that if I had no Propositions to make (for peace with Britain], I would at least give my Advice. I think it is Ariosto who says, that all things lost on Earth are to be found in the

Moon; on which somebody remarked, that there must be a great deal of good Advice in the Moon.

> In a letter to James Hutton, 1 February 1778 (Smyth 7:98–99). The allusion is to Ariosto's *Orlando Furioso*, xxxiv, 68, more familiar from Pope's *Rape of the Lock*, V:113–114: "Some thought it mounted to the Lunar Sphere,/Since all things lost on Earth are treasur'd there"—which carried a note: " *Vid. Ariosto. Canto 34*" (1714 ed., p. 46). The allusion appears in a letter to his sister, 3 June 1786 as "An Italian Poet in his Account of a Voyage to the Moon" (Smyth 9:514).

35.   I suppose you have heard our story of the *harrow*; if not, here it is. A farmer, in our country, sent two of his servants to borrow one of a neighbour, ordering them to bring it between them on their shoulders. When they came to look at it, one of them, who had much wit and cunning, said, "What could our master mean by sending only two men to bring this harrow? No two men upon earth are strong enough to carry it." "Poh!" said the other, who was vain of his strength, "what do you talk of two men? One may carry it. Help it upon my shoulders, and see." As he proceeded with it, the wag kept exclaiming, "Zounds, how strong you are! I could not have thought it. Why, you are a Samson! There is not such another man in America. What amazing strength God has given you! But you will kill yourself! Pray put it down and rest a little, or let me bear a part of the weight." "No, no," said he, being more encouraged by the compliments, than oppressed by the burden; "you shall see I can carry it quite home." And so he did.

> Appended as a note by Jared Sparks to a letter of 24 August 1781 (*Works* [1839] 9:27n), but it seems rather to refer to his appointment as minister plenipotentiary to the French court, 14 September 1778.

36.   When I was a Child of seven Years old, my friends on a Holiday fill'd my little Pocket with Halfpence. I went directly to a Shop where they sold Toys for Children; and being charm'd with the Sound of a Whistle that I met by the way, in the hands of another Boy, I voluntarily offer'd and gave all my Money for it. When I came home, whistling all over the House, much pleas'd with my Whistle, but disturbing all the Family, my Brothers, Sisters and Cousins, understanding the Bargain I had made, told me I had given four times

as much for it as it was worth, put me in mind what good Things I might have bought with the rest of the Money, and laught at me so much for my Folly that I cry'd with Vexation; and the Reflection gave me more Chagrin than the Whistle gave me Pleasure.

> Among the most widely reprinted of BF's anecdotes, this was printed first on his press at Passy in the form of a letter to Mme Brillon, 10 November 1779, with French and English texts on facing pages (rpt., *The Bagatelles from Passy* [New York: Eakins Press, 1967], pp. 125–126).

37.   Such Compliments [from the kings of Denmark and Sweden] might probably make me a little proud, if we Americans were not naturally as much so already as the Porter, who, being told he had with his Burthen jostled the Great Czar Peter (then in London, walking the Street): *"Poh!"* says he, *"we are all Czars here."*

> In "Journal of Negotiations for Peace," about 25 May 1782, recording some of the embarrassments for ambassadors who did not quite know how to treat BF during their visits to Paris (Smyth 8:503).

38.   In what Light we are viewed by superior Beings, may be gathered from a Piece of late West India News, which possibly has not yet reached you. A young Angel of Distinction being sent down to this world on some Business, for the first time, had an old courier-spirit assigned him as a Guide. They arriv'd over the Seas of Martinico, in the middle of the long Day of obstinate Fight between the Fleets of Rodney and De Grasse. When, thro' the Clouds of smoke, he saw the Fire of the Guns, the Decks covered with mangled Limbs, and Bodies dead or dying; the ships sinking, burning, or blown into the Air; and the Quantity of Pain, Misery, and Destruction, the Crews yet alive were thus with so much Eagerness dealing round to one another; he turn'd angrily to his Guide, and said, "You blundering Blockhead, you are ignorant of your Business; you undertook to conduct me to the Earth, and you have brought me into Hell!" "No, Sir," says the Guide, "I have made no mistake; this is really the Earth, and these are men. Devils never treat one another in this cruel manner; they have more Sense, and more of what Men (vainly) call *Humanity*."

> In a letter to his friend of twenty-six years, the Unitarian scientist Joseph Priestley, 7 June 1782, commenting on a current controversy: Admiral Rodney was being taken to task for not

inflicting total punishment on the French ships under the Comte de Grasse after badly beating them just south of Guadalupe, 12 April 1782 (Smyth 8:452–453).

39.   You do well to avoid being concern'd in the Pieces of Personal Abuse, so scandalously common in our Newspapers, that I am afraid to lend any of them here, until I have examined and laid aside such as would disgrace us, and subject us among Strangers to a Reflection like that us'd by a Gentleman in a Coffee-house to two Quarrellers, who, after a mutually free Use of the Words, *Rogue, Villain, Rascal, Scoundrel,* etc. seemed as if they would refer their Dispute to him; "I know nothing of you, or your Affair," said he; "I only perceive *that you know one another.*"

> In a letter to Philadelphia jurist-humorist Francis Hopkinson, 24 December 1782, thanking him for a copy of a playful satire against removing trees from Philadelphia's streets (Smyth 8:647–648). Hopkinson had been the victim of scatological abuse in the Tory papers of New York, and now of vicious attacks by patriotic writers for not responding to the Tories (*Comical Spirit of Seventy-six*, ed. P. M. Zall [1976], pp. 113–130).

40.   I hope we will never deserve, nor any longer appear likely to deserve, the Reproof given to an Enthusiastical Knave in Pennsylvania, who being called upon for an old Debt, said to his Creditors: Thou must have a little more patience; I am not yet able to pay thee. Give me then your bond, says the Creditor, and pay me Interest. No, I cannot do that; I cannot in conscience either receive or pay Interest, it is against my Principle. You have then the Conscience of a Rogue, says the Creditor: You tell me it is against your Principle to Pay Interest; and it being against your Interest to pay the Principal, I perceive you do not intend to pay me either one or t'other.

> In a letter to Samuel Cooper, 26 December 1783, thanking him for news that Massachusetts had just passed an act for helping to pay off the national debt (Smyth 9:145). In the *Worcester Magazine* for July 1786, the story has a British peer saying: "It is not my interest to pay the principal, nor is it my principle to pay the interest" (1:161). BF had used an earlier version in a letter to his sister Jane, 13 January 1772 (P19:28).

The three anecdotes that follow are from BF's pamphlet, "Remarks Concerning the Savages of North America," printed in both French and English on his press at Passy in 1784 and reprinted in English the same year in London along with another pamphlet, "Information to Those Who Would Remove to America," as *Two Tracts*—from which this text derives.

41.   The learning on which we value ourselves, they regard as frivolous and useless. An instance of this occurred at the Treaty of Lancaster in Pennsilvania, anno 1744, between the Government of Virginia and the Six Nations. After the principal business was settled, the Commissioners from Virginia acquainted the Indians by a speech, that there was at Williamsburg a College with a fund, for educating Indian youth, and that if the Chiefs of the Six-Nations would send down half a dozen of their sons to that college, the Government would take care that they should be well provided for, and instructed in all the learning of the white people. It is one of the Indian rules of politeness not to answer a public proposition the same day that it is made; they think it would be treating it as a light matter; and that they shew it respect by taking time to consider it, as of a matter important. They therefore deferred their answer till the day following; when their Speaker began, by expressing their deep sense of the kindness of the Virginia Government, in making them that offer; "for we know," says he, "that you highly esteem the kind of learning taught in those colleges, and that the maintenance of our young men, while with you, would be very expensive to you. We are convinced, therefore, that you mean to do us good by your proposal, and we thank you heartily. But you who are wise must know, that different nations have different conceptions of things; and you will therefore not take it amiss, if our ideas of this kind of education happen not to be the same with yours. We have had some experience of it: Several of our young people were formerly brought up at the colleges of the Northern Provinces; they were instructed in all your sciences; but when they came back to us, they were bad runners, ignorant of every means of living in the woods, unable to bear either cold or hunger; knew neither how to build a cabin, take a deer, or kill an enemy; spoke our language imperfectly; were therefore neither fit for hunters, warriors, or counsellors; they were totally good for nothing. We are however not the less obliged by your kind offer, though we decline accepting

it: and to show our grateful sense of it, if the Gentlemen of Virginia will send us a dozen of their sons, we will take great care of their education, instruct them in all we know, and make *men* of them."

Pages 26–29. Variant of 7.

42.   A Swedish Minister having assembled the Chiefs of the Sasquehanah Indians, made a Sermon to them, acquainting them with the principal historical facts on which our Religion is founded; such as the Fall of our first Parents by eating an Apple; the coming of Christ to repair the mischief; his miracles and suffering, etc.— When he had finished, an Indian Orator stood up to thank him. "What you have told us," says he, "is all very good. It is indeed bad to eat apples. It is better to make them all into cyder. We are much obliged by your kindness in coming so far, to tell us those things which you have heard from your Mothers. In return, I will tell you some of those we have heard from ours.

"In the beginning, our Fathers had only the flesh of animals to subsist on; and if their hunting was unsuccessful, they were starving. Two of our young hunters having killed a deer, made a fire in the woods to broil some parts of it. When they were about to satisfy their hunger, they beheld a beautiful young woman descend from the clouds, and seat herself on that hill which you see yonder among the Blue Mountains. They said to each other, it is a Spirit that perhaps has smelt our broiling venison, and wishes to eat of it: Let us offer some to her. They presented her with the tongue: She was pleased with the Taste of it, and said, your kindness shall be rewarded. Come to this place after thirteen moons, and you shall find something that will be of great benefit in nourishing you and your children to the latest generations. They did so, and to their surprise found plants they had never seen before; but which, from that ancient time, have been constantly cultivated among us, to our great advantage. Where her right hand had touched the ground, they found maize; where her left hand had touched it, they found kidney-beans; and where her backside had sat on it, they found tobacco." The good Missionary, disgusted with this idle tale, said, "What I delivered to you were sacred truths; but what you tell me is mere fable, fiction and falsehood." The Indian, offended, replied, "My Brother, it seems your friends have not done you justice in your education; they have not well instructed you in the rules of common civility. You saw, that we who understand and practise those rules, believed all your stories, why do you refuse to believe ours?"

> Pages 31–33. Variant of *17*. A similar fertility myth in John Bartram's *Travels in Pensilvania and Canada* (1751), pp. 36–37, still flourished among the Senecas in the 1880s (J. Curtin and J. B. Hewitt, "Seneca Fiction, Legends, and Myths," *Bureau of American Ethnology*, 32 [1910–1911]: 652–653).

43.   When the discourse began to flag, the Indian, to continue it, said, "Conrad [Weiser], you have lived long among the white People, and know something of their customs; I have been sometimes at Albany, and have observed, that once in seven days, they shut up their shops, and assemble all in the great house; tell me, what is it for? What do they do there?" "They meet there," says Conrad, "to hear and learn *good things.*" "I do not doubt," says the Indian, "that they tell you so; they have told me the same; But I doubt the truth of what they say, and I will tell you my reasons. I went lately to Albany to sell my skins, and buy blankets, knives, powder, rum, etc. You know I used generally to deal with Hans Hanson; but I was a little inclined this time to try some other Merchants. However, I called first upon Hans, and asked him what he would give for beaver. He said he could not give more than four shillings a pound: But, says he, I cannot talk on business now; this is the day when we meet together to learn *good things*, and I am going to the meeting. So I thought to myself, since I cannot do any business to-day, I may as well go to the meeting too, and I went with him. There stood up a man in black, and began to talk to the people very angrily. I did not understand what he said; but perceiving that he looked much at me, and at Hanson, I imagined he was angry at seeing me there; so I went out, sat down near the house, struck fire, and lit my pipe, waiting till the meeting should break up. I thought too, that the man had mentioned something of Beaver, and I suspected it might be the subject of their meeting. So when they came out, I accosted my Merchant. "Well, Hans," says I, "I hope you have agreed to give more than four shillings a pound." "No," says he, "I cannot give so much. I cannot give more than three shillings and sixpence." I then spoke to several other dealers, but they all sung the same song, three and sixpence, three and sixpence. This made it clear to me that my suspicion was right; and that whatever they pretended of meeting to learn *good*

things, the real purpose was to consult how to cheat Indians in the price of Beaver."

> Pages 36–39. According to P. A. W. Wallace, *Conrad Weiser* (1945), this conversation between Weiser and Chief Canasatego of the Six Nations could have taken place on 17 June 1745 (p. 225). Weiser acted as interpreter for Pennsylvania.

44.   [The People] are pleased with the observation of a Negro, and frequently mention it, that Boccarorra (meaning the white man) make de black man workee, make de horse workee, make de ox workee, make ebery ting workee; only de hog. He de hog, no workee; he eat, he drink, he walk about, he go to sleep when he please, he libb like a Gentleman.

> In "Information to Those Who Would Remove to America," *Two Tracts* (1784), p. 9. The manuscript at Yale contains a concluding sentence that BF did not print: "He no good for nothing until dead; den he bery good—*to cut up*" (R. E. Amacher, *F's Wit & Folly* [1953], p. 156). The anecdote remained popular in jestbooks; for example, *Chaplet of Comus* (1811), p. 248.

45.   [A Gentleman] had built a very fine House, and thereby much impair'd his Fortune. He had a Pride, however, in showing it to his Acquaintance. One of them, after viewing it all, remark'd a Motto over the Door, "ŌIA VANITAS." "What," says he, "is the Meaning of this ŌIA? it is a word I don't understand." "I will tell you," said the Gentleman; "I had in mind to have the Motto cut on a Piece of smooth Marble, but there was not room for it between the Ornaments, to be put in Characters large enough to be read. I therefore made use of a Contraction antiently very common in Latin Manuscripts, by which the *m*'s and *n*'s in Words are omitted, and the Omission noted by a little Dash above, which you may see there; so that the Word is *omnia,* OMNIA VANITAS." "O," says his Friend, "I now comprehend the Meaning of your Motto, it relates to your Edifice; and signifies, that, if you have abridged your *Omnia,* you have, nevertheless, left your VANITAS legible at full length."

> In a letter to his daughter, 26 January 1784, explaining his antipathy to the Society of the Cincinnati who were trying to form an hereditary elite with all the trappings such as mottoes (Smyth 9:167–168). This is a variant of an old jest about Lord

Treasurer Burleigh who "puts a sly squib upon the host" by advising him to make both words the same size—"for OMNIA is very little, and VANITAS exceeding great" (*Merry Passages & Jeasts* [1637-1655], ed. H. F. Lippincott [1974], pp. 44-45; *The Treasury of Wit* [1786], 2:95-96).

46.   A Gentleman in a Coffee-house desired another to sit farther from him. "Why so?" "Because, Sir, you stink," "That is an affront, and you must fight me." "I will fight you, if you insist upon it; but I do not see how that will mend the Matter. For if you kill me, I shall stink too; and if I kill you, [you] will stink, if possible, worse than you do at present."

In a letter to Thomas Percival, English physician and author, thanking him for his latest book and commenting on "the murderous Practice of Duelling" condemned in that book, 17 July 1784 (Smyth 9:237).

47.   The Reverend Commissary Blair, who projected the College of [Virginia], and was in England to solicit Benefactions and a Charter, relates, that the Queen, in the King's Absence, having ordered [Edward] Seymour to draw up the Charter, which was to be given, with £2000 in Money, he oppos'd the Grant; saying that the Nation was engag'd in an expensive War, that the Money was wanted for better purposes, and he did not see the least Occasion for a College in Virginia. Blair represented to him, that its Intention was to educate and qualify young Men to be Ministers of the Gospel, much wanted there; and begged Mr. Attorney would consider, that the People of Virginia had souls to be saved, as well as the People of England. "Souls!" says he, *"damn your Souls. Make Tobacco!"*

In a letter to Marylanders Mason Weems and Edward Gantt then in England seeking ordination in the Anglican Church as Americans, 18 July 1784 (Smyth 9:240). James Blair obtained the charter for the College of William and Mary in 1693 when Seymour was Lord of the Treasury (Parke Rowe, Jr., *James Blair of Virginia* [1971], pp. 70-71). In this letter, BF misrepresents Seymour as "Attorney-General," a mistake thereafter perpetuated by such writers as Winthrop Sargent, *Loyal Verses of Stansbury and Odell* (1860), pp. x-xi, when adopting the jest as their own.

48.   The Skipper of a Shallop, employed between Cape May and Philadelphia, had done us some small Service, for which he

refused Pay. My Wife, understanding that he had a Daughter, sent her as a Present a new-fashioned Cap. Three Years After, this Skipper being at my House with an old Farmer of Cape May, his Passenger, he mentioned the Cap, and how much his daughter had been pleased with it. "But," says he, "it proved a dear Cap to our Congregation." "How so?" "When my Daughter appeared in it at Meeting, it was so much admired, that all the Girls resolved to get such Caps from Philadelphia; and my Wife and I computed, that the whole could not have cost less than a hundred Pound." "True," says the Farmer, "but you do not tell all the Story. I think the Cap was nevertheless an Advantage to us, for it was the first thing that put our Girls upon Knitting worsted Mittens for Sale at Philadelphia, that they might have wherewithal to buy Caps and Ribbands there; and you know that that Industry has continued, and is likely to continue and increase to a much greater Value, and answer better Purposes." Upon the whole, I was more reconciled to this little Piece of Luxury, since not only the Girls were made happier by having fine Caps, but the Philadelphians by the Supply of warm Mittens.

> In a letter to Benjamin Vaughan, his London editor and close friend, 26 July 1784, replying to a query about luxuries in America and suggesting that the hope of obtaining luxuries could be a spur to industry (Smyth 9:243–244). The girls' industry assumes larger significance in view of the fact that New Jersey's manufacturing was stagnant till the Revolution. In 1768 not enough wool was produced "to supply the Inhabitants with Stockings" (*New Jersey Archives*, 10:31).

49.   My Breakfast was a long time Bread and Milk, (no Tea,) and I ate it out of a twopenny earthen Porringer with a Pewter Spoon. But mark how Luxury will enter Families, and make a Progress, in Spite of Principle. Being Call'd one Morning to Breakfast, I found it in a China Bowl with a Spoon of Silver. They had been bought for me without my Knowledge by my Wife, and had cost her the enormous Sum of three and twenty Shillings, for which she had no other Excuse or Apology to make, but that she thought *her* Husband deserv'd a Silver Spoon and China Bowl as well as any of his Neighbours.

> In the *Autobiography*, after describing how much of his early success he had owed to his wife, who shared his inclination to industry and frugality. This passage was written a decade after her death. (NCE p. 350).

50.   [A] Man . . . in buying an Ax of a Smith my Neighbour, desired to have the whole of its Surface as bright as the Edge; the Smith consented to grind it bright for him if he would turn the Wheel. He turn'd while the Smith press'd the broad Face of the Ax hard and heavily on the Stone, which made the Turning of it very fatiguing. The Man came every now and then from the Wheel to see how the Work went on; and at length would take his Ax as it was without farther Grinding. No, says the Smith, Turn on, turn on; we shall have it bright by and by; as yet 'tis only speckled. Yes, says the Man; but—*I think I like a speckled Ax best.*

> In the *Autobiography*, illustrating his willingness to compromise with his inability to acquire better habits of organizing after "much painful Attention" (NCE p. 357). For a variant, see *161*.

51.   How . . . can a Nation, which, among the honestest of its People, has so many Thieves by Inclination, and whose Government encouraged and commissioned no less than 700 Gangs of Robbers; how can such a Nation have the Face to condemn the Crime in Individuals, and hang up 20 of them in a Morning? It naturally puts one in mind of a Newgate Anecdote. One of the Prisoners complain'd, that in the Night somebody had taken his Buckles out of his Shoes; "What, the Devil!" says another, "have we then *Thieves* among us? It must not be suffered; let us search out the Rogue, and pump him to death."

> In a letter to Benjamin Vaughan, 14 March 1785, remarking on the British criminal laws and the practice of privateering (Smyth 9:297).

52.   The Conversations you mention respecting America are pitiable. Those People speak what they wish; but she was certainly never in a more happy Situation. They are angry with us and hate us, and speak all manner of evil of us; but we flourish notwithstanding. They put me in mind of a violent High Church Factor, resident some time in Boston, when I was a Boy. He had bought upon Speculation a Connecticut Cargo of Onions, which he flatter'd himself he might sell again to great Profit, but the Price fell, and they lay upon hand. He was heartily vex'd with his Bargain, especially when he observ'd they began to *grow* in the Store he had fill'd with them. He show'd them one Day to a Friend. "Here they are," says

he, "and they are *growing* too! I damn 'em every day; but I think they are like the Presbyterians; the more I curse 'em, the more they grow."

> In a letter to Jonathan Williams, his nephew and sometime secretary, alluding apparently to rumors in London about America heading for ruin, 19 May 1785 (Smyth 9:329). In its issue for 22 January 1722, the *New-England Courant* had spoken of enemies' attempts to "crush the *Courant*": "These . . . have been attended with their hearty Curses on the *Courant* and its Publishers, but all to no purpose; for, (as a *Connecticut* Trader once said of his Onions,) *The more they are curs'd, the more they grow*" (rpt., *The New-England Courant*, ed. Perry Miller [1956], p. [6]).

53.   But what signifies our Wishing? Things happen, after all, as they will happen. I have sung that *wishing Song*

> [May I govern my Passions with an absolute sway,
> Grow wiser and better as Strength wears away,
> Without Gout or Stone, by a gentle Decay]

a thousand times, when I was young, and now find, at Fourscore, that the three Contraries have befallen me, being subject to the Gout and the Stone, and not being yet Master of all my Passions. Like the proud Girl in my Country, who wish'd and resolv'd not to marry a Parson, nor a Presbyterian, nor an Irishman; and at length found herself married to an Irish Presbyterian Parson.

> In a letter to George Whatley, economist and treasurer of the Foundling Hospital in London, 23 May 1785. The song is Walter Pope's "The Old Man's Wish" (*Oxford Book of 17th Century Verse* [1934], p. 952).

54.   A Surgeon I met with here excused the Women of Paris, by saying, seriously, that they *could not* give suck; "Car," dit il, *"elles n'ont point de tétons."* He assur'd me it was a Fact, and bade me look at them, and observe how flat they were on the Breast; "they have nothing more there," said he, "than I have upon the Back of my hand." I have since thought that there might be some Truth in his Observation, and that, possibly, Nature, finding they made no use of Bubbies, has left off giving them any.

> Ibid. (Smyth 9:334).

55.   You need not be concern'd in writing to me about your bad Spelling: for in my Opinion as our Alphabet now Stands, the bad Spelling, or what is call'd so, is generally the best, as conforming to the Sound of the Letters and of the Words. To give you an Instance, a Gentleman receiving a Letter in which were these Words, Not finding Brown at hom, I delivered your Meseg to his yf. The Gentleman finding it bad Spelling, and therefore not very intelligible, call'd his Lady to help him read it. Between them they pick'd out the meaning of all but the y f, which they could not understand. The lady propos'd calling her Chambermaid; for Betty, says she, has the best Knack at reading bad Spelling of any one I know. Betty came, and was surpriz'd that neither Sir nor Madam could tell what y,f was; why, says she, y,f spells Wife, what else can it spell? And indeed it is a much better as well as shorter method of Spelling Wife, than by Doubleyou,i ef,e, which in reality spells Doubleyifey.

> In a letter to his sister, 4 July 1786 (Carl Van Doren, ed., *The Letters of BF & Jane Mecom* [1950], pp. 273-274). For another jest about phonetic spelling, see *228*.

56.   When I informed your good friend Dr. [Samuel] Cooper, that I was ordered to France, being then seventy years old, and observed, that the public, having as it were eaten my flesh, seemed now resolved to pick my bones, he replied that he approved their taste, for that the nearer the bone the sweeter the meat.

> In a letter to his sister, 4 November 1787 (Ibid., p. 300).

57.   As you observe, there was no swearing in the story of the poker [16], when I told it. The late new dresser of it was, probably, the same, or perhaps akin to him, who, in relating a dispute that happened between Queen Anne and the Archbishop of Canterbury, concerning a vacant mitre, which the Queen was for bestowing on a person the Archbishop thought unworthy, made both the Queen and the Archbishop swear three or four thumping oaths in every sentence of the discussion, and the Archbishop at last gained his point. One present at this tale, being surprised, said, "But did the Queen and the Archbishop swear so at one another?" "O no, no," says the relator; "that is only *my way* of telling the story."

> In a letter to his sister, 26 November 1788 (Ibid., p. 319). The "swearing" version of *16* appeared in the *American Museum* for

August 1788 *(143)* with such additions as "Damn your soul . . . damn me, if I do" etc.

 The next six anecdotes are from the third part of BF's *Autobiography* composed between October 1788 and May 1789. Page references are to the Norton *Anthology of American Literature*, vol. 1 (1979), which reprints the text prepared by P. M. Zall and J. A. Leo Lemay for the Norton Critical Edition series.

58.   [James Logan] told me the following Anecdote of his old Master William Penn respecting Defence. He came over from England, when a young Man, with that Proprietary, and as his Secretary. It was War Time, and their Ship was chas'd by an armed Vessel suppos'd to be an Enemy. Their Captain prepar'd for Defence, but told William Penn and his Company of Quakers, that he did not expect their Assistance, and they might retire into the Cabin; which they did, except James Logan, who chose to stay upon Deck, and was quarter'd to a Gun. The suppos'd Enemy prov'd a Friend; so there was no Fighting. But when the Secretary went down to communicate the Intelligence, William Penn rebuk'd him severely for staying upon Deck and undertaking to assist in defending the Vessel, contrary to the Principles of *Friends,* especially as it had not been required by the Captain. This Reproof being before all the Company, piqu'd the Secretary, who answer'd, *I being thy Servant, why did thee not order me to come down: but thee was willing enough that I should stay and help to fight the Ship when thee thought there was Danger.*

> Page 377. Logan served fifty years after his arrival in 1699 as Penn's agent in Pennsylvania. He was BF's revered friend and cultural patron, giving him access to the library of 3,000 volumes in his home (E. W. Wolf, *Library of James Logan* [1974]).

59.   In the Course of [one of George Whitefield's sermons] I perceived he intended to finish with a Collection, and I silently resolved he should get nothing from me. I had in my Pocket a Handful of Copper Money, three or four Silver Dollars, and five Pistoles in Gold. As he proceeded I began to soften, and concluded to give the Coppers. Another Stroke of his Oratory made me asham'd of that, and determin'd me to give the Silver; and he finish'd so admirably, that I empty'd my Pocket wholly into the Collector's Dish, Gold

and all. At this Sermon there was also one of our Club, who being of my sentiments respecting the Building in Georgia [i.e., where Whitefield planned an orphanage], and suspecting a Collection might be intended, had by Precaution emptied his Pockets before he came from home; towards the Conclusion of the Discourse however, he felt a strong Desire to give, and apply'd to a Neighbour who stood near him to borrow some Money for the Purpose. The Application was unfortunately to perhaps the only Man in the Company who had the firmness not to be affected by the Preacher. His Answer was, *At any other time, Friend Hopkinson, I would lend to thee freely; but not now; for thee seems to be out of thy right Senses.*

> Pages 370–371. "Friend Hopkinson" was Thomas Hopkinson, charter member of BF's Junto and father of Francis Hopkinson mentioned in the note to 39.

60.   The following Instance will show something of the Terms on which we [BF and Whitefield] stood. Upon one of his Arrivals from England at Boston, he wrote to me that he should come soon to Philadelphia, but knew not where he could lodge when there, as he understood his old kind host Mr. [John] Benezet was remov'd for Germantown. My Answer was; You know my House, if you can make shift with its scanty Accommodations you will be most heartily welcome. He reply'd, that if I made that kind Offer for Christ's sake, I should not miss of a Reward.— And I return'd, *Don't let me be mistaken; it was not for Christ's sake, but for your sake.* One of our common Acquaintance jocosely remark'd, that knowing it to be the Custom of the Saints, when they receiv'd any favour, to shift the Burthen of the Obligation from off their own Shoulders, and place it in Heaven, I had contriv'd to fix it on Earth.

> Page 371. This exchange could have taken place for Whitefield's visit of September 1745.

61.   [Commanding soldiers building a fort on the frontier] gave me occasion to observe, that when Men are employ'd they are best contented. For on the Days they work'd they were good-natur'd and chearful; and with the consciousness of having done a good Days work they spent the Evenings jollily; but on the idle Days they were mutinous and quarrelsome, finding fault with their Pork, the Bread, etc. and in continual ill-humour: which put me in mind of a Sea-Captain, whose Rule it was to keep his Men constantly at Work; and

when his Mate once told him that they had done every thing, and there was nothing farther to employ them about; O, says he, *make them scour the Anchor.*

Page 405.

62.   We had for our Chaplain a zealous Presbyterian Minister, Mr. [Charles] Beatty, who complain'd to me that the Men did not generally attend his Prayers and Exhortations. When they enlisted, they were promis'd, besides Pay and Provisions, a Gill of Rum a Day, which was punctually serv'd out to them, half in the Morning and the other half in the Evening, and I observ'd they were as punctual in attending to receive it. Upon which I said to Mr. Beatty, "It is perhaps below the Dignity of your Profession to act as Steward of the Rum. But if you were to deal it out, and only just after Prayers, you would have them all about you." He lik'd the Thought, undertook the Office, and with the help of a few hands to measure out the Liquor executed it to Satisfaction; and never were Prayers more generally and more punctually attended.

Page 405–406.

63.   Going my self one Morning to pay my Respects [to General Loudon, commander of British forces in North America, then in New York], I found in his Antechamber one Innis [George Ennis], a Messenger of Philadelphia, who had come from thence express, with a Pacquet from Governor [William] Denny for the General. He deliver'd to me some Letters from my Friends there, which occasion'd my enquiring when he was to return and where he lodg'd, that I might send some Letters by him. He told me he was order'd to call to-morrow at nine for the General's Answer to the Governor, and should set off immediately. I put my Letters into his Hands the same Day. A Fortnight after I met him again in the same Place. So you are soon return'd, Innis! *Return'd*; No, I am not *gone* yet.— How so?— I have call'd here by Order every Morning these two Weeks past for his Lordship's Letter, and it is not yet ready.— Is it possible, when he is so great a Writer, for I see him constantly at his Scritore. Yes, says Innis, but he is like St. George on the Signs, *always on horseback, and* never rides on.

Page 415. The saying, based on a common tavern sign showing St. George upon a horse with a dragon at its feet, appears also in *Poor Richard's Almanac*, August 1738, and in a letter, 26 June 1755 (P 2:195; 6:87). The meeting with Ennis was in 1757.

64.   I was at the Entertainment given by the City of New York, to Lord Loudon on his taking upon him the Command. Shirley, tho' thereby superseded, was present also. There were a great Company of Officers, Citizens and Strangers, and some Chairs having been borrowed in the Neighbourhood, there was one among them very low which fell to the Lot of Mr. Shirley. Perceiving it as I sat by him, I said, they have given you, Sir, too low a Seat.— No Matter, says he, Mr. Franklin; I find *a low Seat* the easiest!

> Page 417. William Shirley, replaced as commander by Loudon in July 1756, had been governor of Massachusetts since 1741 and had worked with BF on plans for uniting the colonies (V. W. Crane, *BF's Letters to the Presss* [1950], p. xxxix).

65.   [Questioning the effectiveness of a bicameral legislature:] Has not the famous political Fable of the Snake, with two Heads and one Body, some useful Instruction contained in it? She was going to a Brook to drink, and in her Way was to pass thro' a Hedge, a Twig of which opposed her direct Course; one Head chose to go on the right side of the Twig, the other on the left; so that time was spent in the Contest, and, before the Decision was completed, the poor Snake died with thirst.

> In "Queries and Remarks Respecting Alterations in the Constitution of Pennsylvania," replying to an essay in the *Federal Gazette* of 3 November 1789 (Smyth 10:57–58). For variant, see *137*.

66.   'Tis now more than a year since I have heard from my dear friend Le Roy. What can be the reason? Are you still living? or have the mob of Paris mistaken the head of a monopoliser of knowledge, for a monopoliser of corn, and paraded it about the streets upon a pole? . . . Our new constitution is now established, and has an appearance that promises permanency; but in this world nothing can be said to be certain, except death and taxes!

> In a letter to Jean-Baptiste LeRoy, one of BF's earliest supporters among scientists, thirty-six years earlier, and since 1767 a close personal friend in France; 13 November 1789 (*Works of BF* [Philadelphia, 1817], 6:231–232; Smyth 10:68–69).

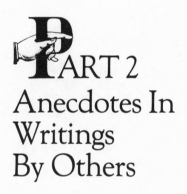

PART 2
Anecdotes In
Writings
By Others

2 | Anecdotes
In Writings
By Others

67. He related a very pleasant accident, which happened to him with this mountain flax [asbestos]: he had, several years ago, got a piece of it, which he gave to one of his journeymen printers, in order to get it made into a sheet at the paper mill. As soon as the fellow brought the paper, Mr. *Franklin* rolled it up, and threw it into the fire, telling the journeyman he would see a miracle, a sheet of paper which did not burn: the ignorant fellow asserted the contrary, but was greatly astonished, upon seeing himself convinced. Mr. *Franklin* then explained to him, though not very clearly, the peculiar qualities of the paper. As soon as he was gone, some of his acquaintance came in, who immediately knew the paper. The journeyman thought he would shew them a great curiosity and astonish them. He accordingly told them that he had curiously made a sheet of paper, which would not burn, though it was thrown into the fire. They pretended to think it impossible, and he as strenuously maintained his assertion. At last they laid a wager about it; but whilst he was busy with stirring up the fire, the others slyly besmeared the paper with fat: the journeyman, who was not aware of it, threw it into the fire, and that moment it was all in flames: this astonished him so much, that he was almost speechless; upon which they could not help laughing, and so discovered the whole artifice.

68. In several houses of the town, a number of little *Ants* run about, living under ground and in holes in the wall. The length of

their bodies is one geometrical line [about 2 cm]. Their colour is either
black or dark red: they have the custom of carrying off sweet things,
if they can come at them, in common with the ants of other countries. Mr. *Franklin* was much inclined to believe that these little
insects could by some means communicate their thoughts or desires
to each other, and he confirmed his opinion by some examples. When
an ant finds some sugar, it runs immediately under ground to its hole,
where having stayed a little while, a whole army comes out, unites and
marches to the place where the sugar is, and carries it off by pieces:
or if an ant meets with a dead fly, which it cannot carry alone, it
immediately hastens home, and soon after some more come out, creep
to the fly and carry it away. Some time ago Mr. *Franklin* put a little
earthen pot with treacle into a closet. A number of ants got into the
pot, and devoured the treacle very quietly. But as he observed it he
shook them out, and tied the pot with a thin string to a nail which
he had fastened in the ceiling; so that the pot hung down by the
string. A single ant by chance remained in the pot: this ant eat till it
was satisfied; but when it wanted to get off, it was under great concern to find its way out: it ran about the bottom of the pot, but in
vain: at last it found after many attempts the way to get to the ceiling
by the string. After it was come there, it ran to the wall, and from
thence to the ground. It had hardly been away for half an hour, when
a great swarm of ants came out climbed up to the ceiling, and crept
along the string into the pot, and began to eat again: this they continued till the treacle was all eaten: in the mean time one swarm
running down the string and the other up.

Peter Kalm, *Travels into North America*, trans. J. H. Foster, 3 vols.
(1770–1771), 1:304–306. A Finnish botanist, Kalm came to America in 1748–1751 to collect plants for the French Academy of
Sciences, and published his book in Stockholm in 1753–1761.
When its English translation appreared, BF complained: "Kalm's
Account of what he learnt in America is full of idle Stories,
which he pick'd up among ignorant People, and either forgetting
of whom he had them, or willing to give them some Authen-
ticity, he has ascrib'd them to Persons of Reputation who never
heard of them till they were found in his Book. And where he
really had Accounts from such Persons, he has varied the Circumstances unaccountably, so that I have been asham'd to meet
with some mention'd as from me. It is dangerous Conversing with
these Strangers that keep Journals" (P 20:96).

69.   Another experiment was to cut through a book of forty eight pages with electricity. Although a bullet might hardly have gone through, the electric "fire" made a fine hole all the way through, just as though a fine knife had been used. The paper was slightly blackened around the hole where the electricity had first entered the book. An electric spark passed through a single sheet of paper so easily that the paper had hardly moved. . . . Franklin had discovered this by chance. It had happened that a lady who had wanted to see Franklin's experiments and had at the same time tried to help him by holding some bottle [battery] had had an electric charge go through her nose. After this she had been under the doctors care for some time. Franklin had tried with thicker piles of paper but then he was not successful. Once there was a hole in the paper the electricity did [not] make a new one but passed through the old one. If the paper was not very big the electricity did not go through it but escaped over the edge.

> Kalm's scientific notebooks, trans. Martti Kerkkonen, *Peter Kalm's North American Journey* (1959), p. 192. Though the notes are confused, it would seem that the lady was injured when BF was experimenting with "thicker piles of paper."

70.   Mr. Soumien [the writer's landlord] had often informed me of great uneasiness and dissatisfaction in Mr. Franklin's family in a manner no way pleasing to me and which in truth I was unwilling to credit, but as Mrs. Franklin and I, of late, began to be Friendly and sociable, I discerned too great grounds for Mr. Soumien's Reflections, arising solely from turbulence and jealousy and pride of her disposition. She suspecting Mr. Franklin for having too great an esteem for his son in prejudice of herself and daughter, a young woman of about 12 or 13 years of age, for whom it was visible Mr. Franklin had no less esteem than for his son. Young Mr. Franklin, I have often seen pass to and from his father's apartment upon Business (for he does not eat, drink or sleep in the House) without least compliment between Mrs. Franklin and him or any sort of notice taken of each other, till one Day as I was sitting with her in the passage when the young Gentleman came by she exclaimed to me (he not hearing):—

"Mr. Fisher, there goes the greatest Villain upon Earth."

This greatly confounded and perplexed me, but did not hinder her from pursuing her Invectives in the foulest terms I ever heard from a Gentlewoman. What to say or do I could not tell, till luckily a neighbor of her acquaintance coming in I made my escape.

> Entry for 28 July 1755 in "Extracts from the Diary of Daniel Fisher," *Pennsylvania Magazine of History and Biography*, 17 (1893): 276–277. An English gentleman who had sought his fortune unsuccessfully in Virginia for two years, Fisher had come to Philadelphia seeking employment with no success. He appealed for help to BF who gave him temporary work as a copyist during May–August. At this time Sarah, or Sally, Franklin was eleven and William, at twenty-four, was comptroller of the general post office and clerk of the Pennsylvania assembly.

71.   Abel James and Doctor Evans drank tea here. Some passages of Benjamin Franklin's droll humor related. In a letter to his sister in New England, a strong Presbyter, [he said]: "I am glad to hear of the reduction of Cape Breton. When it was taken before it was taken by prayer, now by fight, and I desire you will pray that it may never be given up again, which was omitted before." Another: "Your religion leads you three stories high: faith, hope, and charity, but before I go any further, I wish I could turn the house bottom upward and put charity at the bottom."

> Entry for 2 January 1759 in "Extracts from the Diary of Hannah Callender," *Pennsylvania Magazine of History and Biography*, 12 (1888):434. Mrs. Callender, a young Philadelphia Quakeress, kept her diary between 1758–1762. Hers is a weak summary of BF's letter from London to his sister Jane Mecom in Boston, 16 September 1758 (P 8:152–155). The Cape Breton reference is to a family joke—in 1745 BF had warned his brother John that Presbyterian prayers for divine aid in taking Louisbourg could be outweighed by Catholic prayers of the enemy French (P 3:26–27). The confused reference paraphrases this passage in the letter to his sister: "Improvement in Religion, is called *Building Up*, and *Edification. Faith* is then on the Ground-floor, *Hope* is up one Pair of Stairs. My dearly beloved Jenny, don't delight so much to dwell in these lower Rooms, but get as fast as you can into the Garret; for in truth the best Room in the House is *Charity*. For my part, I wish the House was turn'd upside down; 'tis so difficult (when one is fat) to get up Stairs; and not only so, but I imagine *Hope* and *Faith* may be more firmly built on *Charity*, than *Charity* upon *Faith* and *Hope*" (P 8:154).

72.   I was told of a gentleman of Philadelphia, who, in travelling through the provinces of New England, having met with many impertinencies, from this extraordinary turn of character, at length fell upon an expedient almost as extraordinary, to get rid of them. He had observed, when he went into an ordinary [Note: Inns are so called in America.], that every individual of the family had a question or two to propose to him, relative to his history; and that, till each was satisfied, and they had conferred and compared together their information, there was no possibility of procuring any refreshment. He, therefore, the moment he went into any of these places, inquired for the master, the mistress, the sons, the daughters, the men-servants and the maid-servants; and having assembled them all together, he began in this manner. "Worthy people, I am B.F. of Philadelphia, by trade a ———, and a bachelor; I have some relations at Boston, to whom I am going to make a visit; my stay will be short, and I shall then return and follow my business, as a prudent man ought to do. This is all I know of myself, and all I can possibly inform you of; I beg therefore that you will have pity upon me and my horse, and give us both some refreshment."

> Andrew Burnaby, *Travels through the Middle Settlements in North-America, in the Years 1759 and 1760* (1775), pp. 82–83. An English traveler, Burnaby kept detailed accounts of his trip from Virginia to New England. BF's name and trade were spelled out when the anecdote appeared in the *American Museum*, 6 (1789): 205.

73.   Mr. [Edmund] Quincy told a remarkable Instance of Mr. Benjamin Franklin's Activity, and Resolution, to improve the Productions of his own Country, for from that source it must have sprang, or else from an unheard of Stretch of Benevolence to a stranger. Mr. Franklin, happening upon a Visit to his Germantown Friends, to be at Mr. Wiberts Meeting, was asked, after Meeting in the afternoon, to drink Tea, at Mr. Quincy's. The Conversation turned upon the Qualities of American Soils, and the Different Commodities raised in these Provinces. Among the rest, Mr. Franklin mentioned, that the Rhenish Grape Vines had been introduced, into Pennsylvania, and that some had been lately planted in Phyladelphia, and succeeded very well. Mr. Quincy said, upon it, I wish I could get some into my Garden. I doubt not they would do very well in this Province. Mr. Franklin replied, Sir if I can supply you with some of the Cuttings,

I shall be glad to. Quincy thanked him and said, I don't know but some time or other I shall presume to trouble you. And so the Conversation passed off. Within a few Weeks, Mr. Quincy was surprised with a Letter from some of Franklins friends in Boston, that a Bundle of these Rhenish slips were ready for him. These came by Water. Well, soon afterwards he had another Message that another Parcell of slips were left for him by the Post. The next Time Mr. Franklin was in Boston Mr. Quincy waited on him to thank him for his slips, but I am sorry Sir to give you so much Trouble. Oh Sir, says Franklin the Trouble is nothing Sir, to me, if the Vines do but succeed in your Province. However I was obliged to take more Pains than I expected when I saw you. I had been told, that the Vines were in the City but I found none and was obliged to send up to a Village 70 miles from the City for them. Thus he took the Trouble to hunt over the City, and not finding Vines there, he sends 70 miles into the Country, and then sends one Bundle by Water, and least they should miscarry another by Land, to a Gentleman whom he owed nothing, and was but little acquainted with, purely for the sake of Doing Good in the World by Propagating the Rhenish Wines thro these Provinces. And Mr. Quincy has some of them now growing in his Garden. This is an Instance too of his amazing Capacity for Business, His Memory and Resolution. Amidst so much Business as Counsellor, Post Master, Printer, so many private studies, and so many Publick Avocations too, to remember such a transient Hint and exert himself, so in answer to it, is surprising.

> Entry for 26 May 1760, *Diary and Autobiography of John Adams*, ed. L. H. Butterfield, 4 vols. (1961), 1:125–126. In December 1761, BF sent Edmund Quincy a recipe for raisin wine also (P 9:399n).

74.   The Doctor, after having published his method of verifying his hypothesis concerning the sameness of electricity with the matter of lightning, was waiting for the erection of a spire in Philadelphia to carry his views into execution; not imagining that a pointed rod, of a moderate height, could answer the purpose; when it occurred to him, that, by means of a common kite, he could have a readier and better access to the regions of thunder than by any spire whatever. Preparing, therefore, a large silk handkerchief, and two cross sticks, of a proper length, on which to extend it; he took the oppor-

tunity of the first approaching thunder storm to take a walk into a field, in which there was a shed convenient for his purpose. But dreading the ridicule which too commonly attends unsuccessful attempts in science, he communicated his intended experiment to no body but his son, who assisted him in raising the kite.

The kite being raised, a considerable time elapsed before there was any appearance of its being electrified. One very promising cloud had passed over it without any effect; when, at length, just as he was beginning to despair of his contrivance, he observed some loose threads of the hempen string to stand erect, and to avoid one another, just as if they had been suspended on a common conductor. Struck with this promising appearance, he immediately presented his knuc[k]le to the key, and (let the reader judge of the exquisite pleasure he must have felt at that moment) the discovery was complete. He perceived a very evident electric spark. Others succeeded, even before the string was wet, so as to put the matter past all despute, and when the rain had wet the string, he collected electric fire very copiously. This happened in June 1752, a month after the electricians in France had verified the same theory, but before he heard of any thing they had done.

> Joseph Priestley, *History and Present State of Electricity* (1767), pp. 180–181, our only source of information about this experiment. Priestley said his *History* was composed under BF's constant supervision (*Works*, ed. J. T. Rutt, 25 vols. [1817–1832], 1:57–58).

75.   My Affection for the good old Doctor increases every Time I visit him, which I do very frequently. An Anecdote just occurs which will make you smile. Calling t'other Day to ask Dr. Franklin "how he did," I found him sitting, with only a *single* Cap on—the Day was cold—and the Doctor usually wore a *double* one. Upon this, I undertook to remonstrate, and received for Answer, that "his Head grew warm." I said that "Dr. Franklin was never accounted hotheaded." "Aye (says he) but Nature seems to think so, for she is taking all the Hair off my Head."

76.   An hundred other such Things come from him in an Evening. He told me some time ago, that Christians did not debate about the Essentials but about *"the Paper and Packthread of Religion."*

> Letter from London by Thomas Coombe, Jr., to his father, an old friend of BF's, 8 October 1770 (P 17:241).

77.   [During debate on whether states should have representation proportionate to size, Dr. Franklin said] that at the time of the Union between England and Scotland the latter had made the objection which the smaller states now do, but experience had . . . proved that no unfairness had ever been shewn them. that their advocates had prognosticated that it would again happen as in times of old that the whale would swallow Jonas, but he thought the prediction reversed in event and that Jonas had swallowed the whale, for the Scotch had in fact got possession of the government and gave laws to the English.

> Thomas Jefferson, "Notes of Proceedings in the Continental Congress" [7 June to 1 August 1776], (*Papers of TJ*, ed J. P. Boyd [1950-], 1:324). For TJ's variant in 1818, see *245*.

78.   *Lynch* [Thomas Lynch, Jr.] . . . Our slaves being our property, why should they be taxed more than the land, sheep, cattle, horses, etc.? . . .
    Dr. Franklin. Slaves rather weaken than strengthen the State, and there is therefore some difference between them and sheep; sheep will never make any insurrections.

> John Adams's notes on debates in the Continental Congress, 30 July 1776, *Journals*, ed. W. C. Ford, 34 vols. (1904-1937), 6:1080.

79.   Our commissioners returned yesterday after having spent three hours with Lord Howe. . . . In the course of the interview many clever things were said on both sides. When his Lordship asked in what capacity he was to receive them, Mr. [John] Adams said, "In any capacity your Lordship pleases except in that of *British Subjects.*" His Lordship said that nothing would mortify him more than to witness the fall of America and that he would weep for her as for a brother. "I hope," said Dr. Franklin, "your Lordship will be saved that mortification. America is able to take care of herself."

> Letter of Benjamin Rush to his wife, 14 September 1776 (*Letters of BR*, ed. L. H. Butterfield, 2 vols. [1951], 1:109). These remarks do not appear in the commissioners' report read in Congress, 7 September 1776, nor in the minutes kept by the British at the interview. The British reporter had no ear for BF's irony: When Lord Howe was saying Great Britain wished to retain American

it would be more proper to say, Philadelphia had taken Sir William Howe" (2:14). For variants see *127* and *243.*

84.   Having a great desire to be acquainted with Dr. Franklin, this celebrated American was introduced to him. Voltaire accosted and conversed with him some time in English, till Madame Denis interrupted him by saying, that Dr. Franklin understood French, and the rest of the company wished to know the subject of their discourse. "Excuse me, my dear," replied the bard, "I have the vanity to shew, that I am not unacquainted with the language of a Franklin."

85.   An anecdote of Dr. Franklin we will take this opportunity of adding. Since his being at Paris, the Pensylvania stoves, invented by him, are become fashionable; but one of the Ministers being asked whether he would not have one, replied, "By no means—Lord Stormont [British ambassador to France] then will never warm himself at my fire."

"Anecdotes of Voltaire," *Gentleman's Magazine,* 48 (March 1778): 110.

86.   [Dr. William Robertson, Scottish historian] gave me an anecdote, which he had from David Hume. When Dr. Franklin had been at the Board of Trade, upon his first coming to England 20 years ago, Hume said to Mr [James] Oswald, then one of the Lords of Trade, that there had been with them a friend of Hume's, an American, the greatest literary character he had ever known from that part of the world. Oswald said he could not tell what his literary character was, but he was much deceived if he had not enough of the spirit of Faction in him to put a whole Empire into confusion. . . .

87.   Mr [Joseph] Galloway in the coach with me. Among other things he says,— when Dr Franklyn first arrived from England in America, after the revolt was begun, he came to Galloway, they having been long friends; that Galloway opened his mind to him, and hoped he was come to promote a reconciliation: that the Doctor was reserved, and kept upon his guard: that the next morning they met again, and the Doctor said— "Well Mr Galloway, you are really of the mind that I ought to promote a reconciliation?" Galloway said "Yes"— and no more passed: that for five or six weeks Franklyn kept much at home, [and] people seemed at a loss what part he should take. S[amuel] Adams opened against him as a suspicious person,

designing to betray the cause. At length a more full conversation was proposed between F. and G., and the Doctor read to him three fourths of his Journal while he was in England, but company interrupted: that the Doctor's natural son, the Governor of New Jersey, had told Galloway that his father had avoided any conversation with him upon the subject of the colonies; but suspecting his father's intention, the son said to him, he hoped, if he designed to set the Colonies in a flame, he would take care to run away by the light of it: that soon after, Galloway and the two Franklyns met together, and the glass having gone about freely, the Doctor, at a late hour, opened himself, and declared in favour of measures for attaining to Independence:— exclaimed against the corruption and dissipation of the Kingdom, and signified his opinion, that, from the strength of Opposition, the want of union in the Ministry, the great resources in the Colonies, they would finally prevail. He urged Galloway to come into the Congress again; and from that time, united in the closest connection with Adams, broke off with Galloway, who lost the remaining part of his Journal, which probably was the most interesting. Galloway remembers Franklyn told him a plan was laid for stopping him in England, which a friend of great character in the law gave him notice of, and that he gave out he should sail in a fortnight by the packet, but went off suddenly by another opportunity. . . .

88.   It seems agreed Franklin is now sole Minister from the revolted Colonies. Mr [William] Straham, the King's Printer, and now member of Parliament for [Malmesbury] told me what I did not know before— that soon after Franklin was of age, he procured by his labour, money enough to pay his passage from Philadelphia to London, where he supported himself 18 months by working as a Pressman in a Printing house in Wild Court, near Lincolns Inn Fields. After Franklin came over Agent for Pensylvania, he proposed several times to Strahan [who had worked with him there], to go and make a visit to his old master [John] Watts, who was then living, but something or other was always in the way.

> Entries for 24 March 1778, 6 January, and 19 March 1779 in the diary of Massachusetts Governor Thomas Hutchinson, then exiled in London, ed. P. O. Hutchinson, *Diary and Letters of Thomas Hutchinson*, 2 vols. (1885–1886), 2:237–238, 246–247.

89.   Dr. Franklin being mentioned, my lord [Mansfield] said that he [BF] carried his grandson (which, by the way, is the natural son of his natural son, both by street women) to Voltaire, who said to the Boy — *Love God and Liberty.*

> Entry for 29 August 1779, in Governor Hutchinson's diary, rpt., P. Hutchinson in *Notes and Queries*, 4 ser., 5 (1870):70, where it differs from the version in the edition cited in 88. That edition had a note: "The Editor has here omitted a few words in a parenthesis. They concern genealogy rather than history" (2:278n). Those words could have been common gossip or a faulty echo of a piece in the London *Morning Post*, 1 June 1779, saying William Franklin was BF's son "by an oyster wench in Philadelphia, whom he left to die in the streets of disease and hunger." For another echo, see 167. For variant reports on Voltaire's blessing, bestowed in February 1778, see 169 and 201.

90.   Dr. [William] Robertson, the Historian, told me on the 5th that he knew Franklin well, who had been thrice in Scotland several years ago. Being once at Scone and told it was there the old Scottish Kings had used to be crowned, Franklin said, "Who knows but St. James's may some time or other lie in ruins as Scone does now,"— a commonplace reflection, if what has since happened did not make it memorable, and indicate how long he had harboured his plan.

> Journal of Horace Walpole for April 1778, ed. John Doran, *Journals of the Reign of King George the Third*, 2 vols. (1859), 2:251. The London *Political Magazine* for October 1780 varies this by having BF say: "We are now treading on the ruins of antient palaces; perhaps our descendants may do the same in future days at St. James's, and say, here formerly stood the palace of the Kings" (1:633).

91.   A wit at dinner [in 1776] said to Franklin, "One must admit, monsieur, that it is a great and superb spectacle which America offers us today." "Yes," replied Franklin modestly, "but the spectators do not pay."

> Frédéric-Melchior von Grimm's newsletter, *Correspondence Littéraire*, July 1778, trans. A. O. Aldridge, *F and His French Contemporaries* (1957), p. 188.

92.   A gentleman just returned from Paris informs us that Dr. Franklin has shaken off entirely the mechanical rust, and commenced the complete courtier. Being lately in the gardens of Versailles, showing the Queen some electrical experiment, she asked him, in a fit of raillery, if he did not dread the fate of Prometheus, who was so severely served for stealing fire from Heaven? "Yes, please your majesty," (replied old Franklin with infinite gallantry), "if I did not behold a pair of eyes this moment which have stolen infinitely more fire from Jove than ever I did, pass unpunished though they do more mischief in a week than I have done in all my experiments."

> London Chronicle, 7 July 1778, rpt., New Hampshire Gazette,
> 22 December 1778 (Carl Van Doren, ed., Letters of BF and Jane
> Mecom [1950], p. 191). His sister teased him: "Bless God I now
> and then hear of your health and glorious Achievements in the
> political way, as well as in the favour of the Ladys (Since you have
> rubd off the Mechanic Rust and commenced compleat courtier)"
> (ibid., p. 192). The story remained popular in jestbooks and
> periodicals; for example, Niles Register, 1 August 1829, p. 366.

93.   Dr. Franklyn was bred a printer, and followed this profession for some time in Boston, but possessing too liberal a spirit at that time for the meridian of that city, he was obliged to quit it abruptly, and fly to Philadelphia. Being much narrowed in his circumstances, he was obliged to walk all the way to the last-mentioned place, where, being arrived just at the time that the congregation were going to morning service, young Franklyn mixed with the croud, and, perhaps partly from the benefit of getting a seat to sit down on, attended divine service.

Oppressed with too much fatigue, he had not been long there, when he fell asleep, and continued so, after the service was over, till the sexton, just going to lock the door, perceiving his situation, woke him. Franklyn on this immediately got up, *unknowing where to go, or what to do.*

At last a wealthy citizen of Philadelphia, seeing him a stranger, and perhaps seeing that perturbation of mind in his face which such a situation as his generally paints, he asked him, "Whether he was not a stranger? How long had he been in town, etc." To these questions Franklyn gave such ingenious and modest answers, that the citizen asked him home to dinner with him; the consequence of which visit was, that liking his conversation, and above all, the openness

of his manner, and the enterprise of his spirit, he made out an appointment for him in his own family, and there having the benefit of
seeing and conversing with some of the principles of that city, he pro-
gressively laid the foundation of his present exalted situation.

> *London Chronicle*, 1 October 1778, rpt., A. O. Aldridge, "First
> Published Memoir of F," *William and Mary Quarterly*, 3d ser.,
> 24 (1967): 624–625. This odd mixture of fact and fancy may
> derive from someone having heard BF tell, as he does in the
> *Autobiography* (not yet then circulating), how he was befriended
> by the printer William Bradford of New York who sent him on
> to his son in Philadelphia, Andrew Bradford, with whom he
> lived—after first falling asleep during a Quaker meeting.

94.   At the end of some years he took a fancy to go and settle
in Philadelphia, which being a more considerable city than Boston,
he hoped he should sooner find the means of making his fortune.
Being still young when he arrived at Philadelphia, he soon spent all
the money he had saved at Boston, and was obliged to engage with
a printer there, with whom he lived four years. During this interval
he contrived to amass the sum of sixty guineas; when growing weary
of his trade, and having in his physical researches made an important
discovery; namely, that for four-pence a day a man may provide
himself with diet, lodging, and every other necessary. "Well," said he,
"the money which I have laid by will carry me on a long time, as I
can be contented with so small an income."— He then quitted his
master, and lived privately, subsisting for many years upon four-pence
a day. . . .
        His method was (for I have taken him for my pattern) to
purchase for three-pence a quantity of potatoes, which served him
for bread and meat both, and of which there was sufficient to subsist on a whole week. A baker roasted them for a half-penny; and
he bought of a milk-woman daily a half-penny worth of milk; all this
amounted to no more than seven pence a week; he gave a penny a
day for his lodgings in a garret, because he liked neatness and convenience, otherwise he might have accommodated himself at a cheaper
rate. He drank small beer mixed with water, and this cost him twopence a week; the remainder he laid by for dress and pocket-money;
for he employed nobody to wash for him, or to mend his linen and
stockings.

History of a French Louse (London, 1779), translation of a French political satire, pp. 60–61. As in 93, the story seems to echo the *Autobiography* but the details are fanciful. BF had read his draft of the *Autobiography* to friends in England in 1771, but at this time the draft was lost to him, hidden in Philadelphia. I imagine that this kind of story derived from BF's recitation, subsequently distorted in passing by word of mouth.

95.   Mr. Z. [Ralph Izard] while at Paris had often pressed the Doctor to communicate to him his several negociations with the court of France which the Doctor avoided as decently as he *could.* At length he received from Mr. Z. a very intemperate letter. He folded it up and put it into a pigeon hole. A second, third and so on to a fifth or sixth he received and disposed of in the same way. Finding no answer *could* be obtained by letter Mr. Z. paid him a personal visit and gave a loose to all the warmth of which he is susceptible. The Doctor replied I can no more answer this conversation of yours than the several impatient letters you have written me (taking them down from the pigeon hole). Call on me when you are cool and goodly humoured and I will justify myself to you. They never saw each other afterwards.

> Code letter by Thomas Jefferson to James Madison, 31 January 1783, as an exercise in using the code—decoded by Julian P. Boyd, ed., *Papers of TJ* (1952–), 6:225–26. Ralph Izard busily impeded the mission until Congress ordered him home in 1779.

96.   Commodore [George] Johnstone, Doctor Franklin, and others, passed a day, many years since, about Maidenhead. In the course of the afternoon the company separated, and the Doctor was found in a reverie, looking on the Thames. Being asked what was the object of his contemplation: "I am musing (he replied) on the improper distribution of power, and lamenting that the noble rivers in America should be subject to the paltry stream I am now beholding."

> *Scots Magazine,* 45 (April 1783): 175n.

97.   While the Doctor was under examination, Counsellor W[edderburne] (Now Lord L[oughborough]) treated him with utmost indignity, in short he used the language of an insolent Scotchman, which the philosopher bore with the serenity of a man of good sense insulted by an object of contempt. After his examination, it is said,

he passed by the Counsellor, in his way out, and took occasion to whisper the follow truth in his ear—*I will make your master a LITTLE KING for this.*

> *European Magazine* (London), 3 (March 1783): 165. The setting is BF's "trial" in the Privy Council, 1774, when he was abused for circulating the private correspondence of Governor Hutchinson, and subsequently removed as postmaster general for North America. For other anecdotes about the trial, see *111* and *128*.

98.　　　　Many people who prided themselves upon remaining indifferent [to the first ballon flights] in the midst of public enthusiasm did not fail to repeat, "To what use do they expect to put these experiments? What good is this discovery that they make so much noise about?" The venerable Franklin replied with his accustomed simplicity, "What good is a new-born baby?"

> Baron Frédéric-Melchior von Grimm, *Correspondance Littéraire* for August 1783, trans. A. O. Aldridge, *F and His French Contemporaries*, p. 188. BF's own reports of the balloon flights are in a letter to Sir Joseph Banks, 30 August 1783 (Smyth 9:79–85).

 The following five anecdotes are from the journal of John Baynes (1759–1787), a young Englishman who visited Passy in 1783, printed in John Bigelow, ed., *Works of BF* (1887), 8:410–425.

99.　　　　I observed how some of our papers had affected to depreciate [Washington's] motive in retiring, and added that I should always suppose a man to act from good motives till I saw cause to think otherwise. "Yes," said he, "so would every honest man"; and then he took an opportunity of reprobating the maxim that all men were equally corrupt. "And yet," said Mr. [Samuel] Romilly, "that was the favorite maxim of Lord North's administration." Dr. Franklin observed that such men might hold such opinions with some degree of reason, judging from themselves and the persons they knew. "A man," added he, "who had seen nothing but hospitals, must naturally have a poor opinion of the health of mankind."

> Pages 411–412.

100.   I proceeded to Dr. Franklin's house. On entering a confounded Swiss servant told me to go up stairs and I should meet with
domestics. I went up, but not a domestic was there; I returned and
told him there was nobody. He then walked up with me, and pointing to the room before me, told me I might enter, and I should find
his master alone. I desired him to announce me. "O Monsieur, c'est
pas nécessaire; entrez, entrez!" on which I proceeded, and, rapping at
the door, I perceived that I had disturbed the old man from a sleep
he had been taking on a sofa. My confusion was inexpressible. However, he soon relieved me from it, saying that he had risen early that
morning, and that the heat of the weather had made a little rest not
unacceptable.

Pages 413–414.

101.   Walked to Passy to see Dr. Franklin, but took care to make
the servant announce me regularly. Found him with some American
gentlemen and ladies, who were conversing upon American commerce, in which the ladies joined. On their departure I was much
pleased to see the old man attend them down stairs and hand the
ladies to their carriage. On his return I expressed my pleasure in hearing the Americans, and even the ladies, converse entirely upon commerce. He said that it was so throughout the country; not an idle
man, and consequently not a poor man, was to be found.

Page 417.

102.   I likewise mentioned Dr. [Richard] Price's plan for a general peace in Europe . . . "I will, however," continued he, "mention
one plan to you, which came to me in rather an extraordinary manner, and which seems to me to contain some very sensible remarks.
In the course of last year, a man [Pierre-André Gargaz] very shabbily
dressed—all his dress together was not worth five shillings—came
and desired to see me. He was admitted, and, on asking his business,
he told me that he had walked from one of the remotest provinces
in France, for the purpose of seeing me and showing me a plan which
he had formed for a universal and perpetual peace. I took his plan
and read it, and found it to contain much good-sense. I desired him to
print it. He said he had no money; so I printed it for him. He took
as many copies as he wished for, and gave several away; but no notice

whatever was taken of it." He then went into a closet and brought a copy of this plan, which he gave me.

> Pages 418–419. BF's own version of this episode is in his letter to David Hartley, 10 July 1782 (Smyth 8:564–565). The book was Pierre-André Gargaz, *Project of Universal and Perpetual Peace*, rpt. G. S. Eddy (New York, 1922).

103.   [BF said:] "I remember dining at a nobleman's house where they were speaking of a distant relation of his who was prevented from marrying a lady whom he loved, by the smallness of their fortunes; everybody was lamenting their hard situation, when I took the liberty to ask the amount of fortunes. 'Why,' said a gentleman near me, 'all they can raise between them will scarce be £40,000.' I was astonished; however, on recollecting myself, I suggested that £40,000 was a pretty handsome fortune; that it would, by being vested in the Three Per Cents, bring in £1,200 a year. 'And pray, sir, consider, what is £1,200 a year? There is my lord's carriage and my lady's carriage, etc. etc.' So he ran up £1,200 in a moment. I did not attempt to confute him; but only added that, notwithstanding all he had said, if he would give me the £40,000, I would endow 400 American girls with it, every one of whom should be esteemed a fortune in her own country.

> Page 421.

 The next six anecdotes are from *Conversations of Dr. Franklin and Mr. Jay*, recorded by John Jay while living with BF at Passy in 1783–1784, ed., Frank Monaghan (1936).

104.   Robert Hunter Morris . . . who for about a Year was Governor of Pennsylvania, the Doctor knew very well— It seems that the Doctor was at New York on his Way to Boston when Morris arrived there from England. He asked the Doctor many Questions about Pennsylvania, about the Temper of the People, and whether he thought it difficult for him to pass his Time agreable among them— The Doctor told him nothing would be more easy if he avoided disputes with the Assembly— but replied he laughingly, *why would you have me deprive myself of one of my greatest pleasures*— he was fond of disputing and thought he had Talents for it— However added he I

will take your advice— on Franklin's return from Boston to Philadelphia he found the Governor and Assembly in warm altercations—
the Doctor was a member of the Assembly, and was appointed to
Draw up their answer— Morris after having sent a Message to the
assembly, met Samuel Rhodes and asked him what he thought of it—
Rhodes said he thought it very smart— ah said Morris I thought so
too when I had finished it— but tomorrow we shall see Benjamin
Franklin's answer and then I suspect we shall both change our Minds—
Although he knew that Franklin conducted the dispute against him—
yet they were always good friends, and frequently dined together etc.—

> Pages 11–12. Like *107* and *108* this story prefigures episodes in
> the portion of the *Autobiography* that BF composed in 1788 (NCE
> pp. 391–392).

105.   The elder Lewis Morris was brought up by an Uncle—
when young he was very wild— his Uncle sent him to the West Indies
with a Vessel and Cargo, which he spent— on his Return he married—
his Uncle observed to him on that occasion "that now when he
wanted everything he got himself a Wife" he replied that now he did
not want everything,— his Uncle asked him what it was that he did
not want— he answered that *now he did not want a Wife*— Dr. Franklin
was told this by some of Morris's Cotemporaries.

> Page 12.

106.   Dr. Franklin lived at Philadelphia in the Neighbourhood
of Mr. Boudinot the Father of Elias Boudinot the present President
of Congress— the Father was a Silver Smith who had come from
New York to settle at Philadelphia, a Man much devoted to [George]
Whitfield, by whom his Son was baptized *Elias* after the Prophet of
that Name— Dr Franklin remembers Elias coming to his Father's
Door with half a Water Melon and a Spoon in his Hand— several
of the neighboring Boys gathered round in Hopes of sharing in the
Melon— Elias observed their Intention, but told them as they came
up, that those who asked should receive nothing, and went on eating
his Melon— The others imagining he meant to Share with them, and
fearing to ask lest they should as he threatned be refused, silently
waited his Motions— he went on however eating his Melon, and
finished it— He was eight or nine Years old—

> Page 13.

107.   Doctor Franklin, who has lived long and much with Quakers, tells me that he thinks the far greater part of them approve of defensive though not of offensive War. In the Course of the War which ended in 1748— It was thought necessary to erect a Battery at Philadelphia and a Lottery was made to defray part of the Expence— at that Time the Doctor was of a fire Company of thirty Members, twenty-two of whom were Quakers— they had sixty pounds of public or Company Stock— and the Doctor proposed to lay it out in Lottery Tickets— it was their Custom in all Money Matters to give Notice or make the Motion a Week before its Determination— When the Doctor moved his Proposition Anthony Morris a Quaker Member opposed it strenuously observing that the Friends could not apply Money to Purposes of War and that if the Doctor persisted in this motion, it would be the Means of breaking up the Company— the Doctor observed that the Minority must be bound by the Majority, and as the greater part of the Company were Quakers it would be in their power to decide as they pleased. When the Day for the Determination came, Anthony Morris was the only Quaker who appeared— the Doctor observing that Circumstance pressed for the Vote— Morris said he expected that other Members would soon come [in], and begging that the Vote might be deferred for an Hour— While that matter was in agitation, the Waiter called him out, Telling him that two Men below Stairs wanted to Speake to him— he found they were two Quaker Members of the Company— They told him they came from six or seven others who were in a Home next Door but one— they came to inquire whether he was strong enough to carry his Motion— if not that on being sent for they would attend and vote with him— but they wished to avoid it if possible lest they should give offence to certain of the Friends who were more scrupulous on that Head— The Doctor returned and agreed to Anthony Morris's Request for another Hour— the Hour elapsed and not a single Quaker appeared— the Question was then put and carried.

> Pages 13–14. See the *Autobiography* for BF's own version of this episode (NCE p. 376).

108.   While Governor [George] Thomas was Governor of Pennsylvania shortly after the taking of Louisbourgh by an armament from Boston, advice came to Philadelphia that the Garrison was in great want of Gun powder— Governor Thomas communicated it to the Assembly and wanted them to afford Supplies the Quaker majority in

the Assembly would not consent to supply any Gun powder— but they granted three thousand pounds to be laid out in Flour Wheat or other *Grain* for the use of the Garrison— Governor Thomas said that by *other Grain* was meant Gun Powder— he laid the Money out accordingly and nothing was said about it—

> Pages 14–15. See the *Autobiography* for BF's own version (NCE p. 377–378).

109.   Doctor Franklin told me that the Quaker Morris Family of Philadelphia are descended from Anthony Morris a Quaker who came there from England about the Beginning of this Century— It was said among the old People, that he was a natural Son of a Spanish Embassador in England— the Doctor says he always thought he looked a little like a Spaniard— He was an industrious money getting Man, as well as a rigid Quaker— He once found a friend of his reading a large Book— What, says he, *art thee reading that Book? Why a Man might earn forty Shillings in the Time necessary to read it through*—

> Page 15.

110.   This lady [Mme Helvétius] I dined with at Dr. Franklin's. She entered the room with a careless, jaunty air; upon seeing ladies who were strangers to her, she bawled out, "Ah! mon Dieu, where is Franklin? Why did you not tell me there were ladies here?" You must suppose her speaking all this in French. "How I look!" said she, taking hold of a chemise made of tiffany, which she had on over a blue lutestring, and which looked as much upon the decay as her beauty, for she was once a handsome woman; her hair was frizzled; over it, she had a small straw hat, with a dirty gauze half-handkerchief round it, and a bit of dirtier gauze, than ever my maids wore, was bowed on behind. She had a black gauze scarf thrown over her shoulders. She ran out of the room; when she returned, the Doctor entered at one door, she at the other; upon which she ran forward to him, caught him by the hand, "Hélas! Franklin;" then gave him a double kiss, one upon each cheek, and another upon his forehead. When we went into the room to dine, she was placed between the Doctor and Mr. [John] Adams. She carried on the chief of the conversation at dinner, frequently locking her hand into the Doctor's, and sometimes spreading her arms upon the backs of both the gentlemen's chairs, then throwing her arm carelessly upon the Doctor's neck.

I should have been greatly astonished at this conduct, if the good Doctor had not told me that in this lady I should see a genuine Frenchwoman, wholly free from affectation or stiffness of behaviour, and one of the best women in the world. For this I must take the Doctor's word; but I should have set her down for a very bad one, although sixty years of age, and a widow. I own I was highly disgusted, and never wish for an acquaintance with any ladies of this cast. After dinner she threw herself upon a settee, where she showed more than her feet. She had a little lap-dog, who was, next to the Doctor, her favorite. This she kissed, and when he wet the floor, she wiped it up with her chemise. This is one of the Doctor's most intimate friends, with whom he dines once every week, and she with him.

> Letter from Abigail Adams to her sister from France, 5 September 1784, ed., C. F. Adams, *Letters of Mrs. Adams*, 4th ed. (1848), pp. 199–200. Her daughter, Abby, noted the same event in her own journal, 1 September 1784: "Dined at Dr. Franklin's invitation; a number of gentlemen, and Mme Helvetius, a French lady 60 years of age. Odious indeed do our sex appear when divested of those ornaments, with which modesty and delicacy adorn them" (Abigail Adams Smith, *Journal and Correspondence*, 2 vols. [1841–1842], 1:17).

111.   The scene [of signing the Anglo-American peace treaty] was it seems, to be at Dr. Franklin's house. For just as the great deliverer of the Colonies from their enslavement to the notorious tyranny of Great Britain, appeared in the act to set his august hand to the blessed instrument of a peace of his own dictating, he stopped short on a sudden; checked, as might be supposed, by a secret remorse at the horrid crime he was about to perpetuate.— Nothing like it.— He begs of the parties present to retire for a few minutes. He leaves the room, and presently returns; when having asked them whether they could guess the motives of his short eclipse, and being answered in the negative, the traitor, with such a malignant grin as may be imagined of a fiend of hell on his having accomplished some mischief worthy of a damned spirit, satisfied his hearers in these or the like terms:

"Gentlemen, I beg pardon for having detained you, but mark this coat.— *We do, and observe that it is the same in which you left the room!* No, it is not; but at the point of my disseevering the British empire, I could not refuse to myself the plenary enjoyment of my triumph on the glorious occasion; accordingly I now sign these decisive articles of separation in the very coat that I wore at the time when Mr. [Alexander] Wedderburne abused me at the Council Chamber; an indignity which I rejoice thus to revenge on his master, and the whole British nation."

> Letter in the London *Public Advertiser*, signed "A Briton," 11 July 1785, which confused the signing of the British treaty of 1783 with that of the treaty with France in 1778— see *128* and *204*. In the next issue of the *Public Advertiser*, the story was denied by Caleb Whitfoord, who had been secretary of the British commissioners and an eyewitness at the signing. BF thanked Whitfoord for this defense, adding: "It is hardly worth while to let him know, that the Person he is so desirous of defaming, not only did not mention the Transaction he alludes to, at the time he states, but at no other time, nor to any other Person or Persons, from the Day it happen'd to the present" (Smyth 9:605–606).

112.   Immediately after brakefast I went by perticular Invitation to spend the Day with Doctor Franklin— I found him in his little Room Among his Papers— he received me very politely and immediately entered into conversation about the Western Country— his Room makes a Singular Appearance, being filled with old philosophical Instruments, Papers, Boxes, Tables, and Stools— About 10 OClock he sat some water on the fire and not being expert through his great age I desired him to give me the pleasure of assiting him, he thanked me and replied that he ever made it a point to wait upon himself and although he began to find himself infirm he was determined not to encrease his Infirmities by giving way to them— After his water was hot I observed his Object was to shave himself which Operation he performed without a Glass and with great expedition— I asked him if he never employed a Barber he answered, "no" and continued nearly in the following words "I think happiness does not consist so much in perticular pieces of good fortune that perhaps accidentally fall to a Mans Lot as to be able in his old age to do those little things which was he unable to perform himself would be done by others with a sparing hand—"

> Entry for 4 December 1785, diary of Andrew Ellicott, one of the surveyors of the Mason-Dixon Line, ed. C. V. Mathews, *Andrew Ellicott His Life and Letters* (1908), pp. 50–51. In that portion of the *Autobiography* composed about December 1788,

BF says: "Human Felicity is produc'd not so much by great Pieces of good Fortune that seldom happen, as by little Advantages that occur every Day. Thus if you teach a poor young Man to shave himself and keep his Razor in order, you may contribute more to the Happiness of his Life than in giving him 1000 Guineas" (NCE pp. 388–389).

 Anecdotes *113* through *129* are from the manuscript notebooks of Benjamin Rush in the Pennsylvania Historical Society, "Letters, Facts and Observations upon a Variety of Subjects" (Yi 2/2/7262, vols. 3 and 4). All but *129* are consecutive in vol. 3, pp. 175–185, headed "Conversations with Dr Franklin"; *129* is in vol. 4, pp. 77–78. They had been previously printed in the *Pennsylvania Magazine of History and Biography*, 29 (1905): 24–29, and in G. W. Corner, ed., *Autobiography of Benjamin Rush* (1948), pp. 171–212. But the text below derives from a microfilm of the notebooks, retaining Rush's idiosyncracies.

113.   1785. . . . He said the foundation of the American revolution was laid in 1733, by a clause in a bill to subject the Colonies to being governed by royal instructions which was rejected.— He said in 1765 when he went to England he had a long conversation with Mr [Charles] Pratt (afterwards Lord Camden) who told him that Britain would drive the colonies to independance. This he said first led him to realize its occurring shortly.

114.   1786 August: . . . He said he believed that Tabacco would in a few years go out of Use— That about 30 years ago when he went to England smoking was universal in taverns, coffe houses, and private families— but that it was now generally laid aside— that the use of Snuff— from being universal in France was become unfashionable among genteel people— no person of fashion under 30 years of age now snuffed in France. He added that Sir John Pringle and he had observed that tremors of the hands were more frequent in France than elsewhere, and probably from the excessive use of Snuff. They once saw in a company of 16 but two persons who had not these tremors at a table in France. He said Sir John was cured of a tremor by leaving off Snuff. He concluded that there was no great advantage

in using Tabacco in any way, for that he had kept company with persons who used it all his life, and no one had ever advised him to use it. The Doctor in the 81st year of his age declared he never had snuffed— chewed— or smoked.—

115.   September 23rd: . . . He said he believed the Accounts of the plague in Turkey were exaggerated. He once conversed with a Dr McKensie who had resided 38 years at Constantinople, who told him there were *five* plagues in that town. The plague of the drugger men or interpreters who spread false Stories of the prevalence of the plague in order to drive foreign ministers into the Country in order that they might enjoy a little leisure. 2 The plague of debtors who when dunned, looked out of their Windows, and told their creditors, not to come in for the plague is in their houses. 3 The plague of the Doctors— for as they are never paid for their Attendance on such patients as die, Unless it be with the plague, they make most of the *fatal* diseases the plague.— The Doctor forgot the other two. He added that Dr Mackensie upon hearing that 660 dead with the plague, were carried out of one of the gates daily, had the curiosity to stand by that gate for one whole day, and counted only 66.—

116.   1787 May 3rd: drank tea with Dr. Franklin— he spoke in high terms against negro Slavery— and said he printed a book 40 years ago [*All Slavekeepers . . . Apostates* (1738)] by Benjamin Lay against it, which though confused, contained just thoughts and good sense but in bad order.

117.   April— dined with Ditto. He spoke of the talkativeness of the French nation, and told a story of the Abbe Raynal— who was a great talker who came into a Company where a french man talked so long and so incessantly that he could not get in a word— at last he cried out "il e perdu— si il crache" "he is lost— if he spits"— His grandson told another story of a frenchman who was dining complaining to his companions that their noise kept him from tasting his Victuals.

118.   1788 April 19th— spent half an hour with Dr Franklin in his library. "He observed that a man lost 10 per cent on the *value*, by lending his books— that he once knew a man who never returned a borrowed book, because no one ever returned books borrowed from him"—

119.   He condemned the *foreign* commerce of the United States, and observed that the greatest part of the trade of the World was carried on for Luxuries most of which were really injurious to health or Society— such as *tea*— *Rum*— *Sugar*— and *negro Slaves*. He added— "when I read the Advertisements in our papers of imported goods for sale— I think of the Speech of a philosopher upon walking through a fair "how happy am I that I want none of these things."—

A letter of 19 August 1771 alludes to this saying (P18:210).

120.   September 22. . . . The Doctor said few but quacks ever made money by physic, and that no bill drawn upon the credulity of the people of London by quacks was ever protested. He ascribed the success of quacks partly to patients extolling the efficacy of the remedies they took from them, rather than confess their ignorance and credulity—hence it was justly said "quacks were the greatest lyars in the world, except their patients."

121.   He told two Stories— the one of a Jew who had peculated in the french army, being told when under confinement that he would be hanged— to which the Jew answered "who ever heard of a man being hanged worth 200,000 livres"— and he accordingly escaped.

122.   The Judges in Mexico being ordered to prosecute a man for peculation found him innocent, for which they said "they were sorry both for his own, and their sakes."

123.   He added further— that in riding through new England, he overtook a post Rider that was once a Shoemaker— and fell into consumption— but upon riding two years as a post in all weathers between New York, and Connecticut river (140 miles) he recovered perfectly— Upon which he returned to his old business, but upon finding a return of his consumption, he rode post again— in which business he continued in good health 30 years.—

124.   He said that he could have *purchased* the independance of America at one-tenth of the money expended in defending it— such was the Venality of the British Court.

For an expanded variant, see *163*.

125.   1789 June 12th— Had a long conversation with him on the latin and greek languages. He called them the "quackery" of literature.

He spent only about a year at a latin School, when between 8 and 9 years of Age. At 33, he learned french— after this Italian and Spanish which led him to learn latin which he acquired with great ease.—

> BF's explanation of how he learned Latin this way is in the *Autobiography* (NCE p. 365).

126.   He highly approved of learning Geography in early life— and said that he had taught himself it, when a boy while his father was at prayers by looking over four large maps which hung in his father's parlour.—

> This is followed in Rush's notebook by three memoranda: "Time misspent— and time spending itself.—" "Four ways of winding up Conversations— by Stories of robbers— Duels— murders and in America of Snakes.—" "The ministry read history not to avoid blunders, but to adopt and imitate them.—"

127.   "So (said Mr Gerard)— Sir William Howe has taken Philadelphia—" "you mean Sir Philadelphia has taken Sir William Howe."

> "Mr Gerard" was most likely Conrad Alexandre Gérard, named France's minister to America in 1778. Variant of *83* and *243*.

128.   Why do you wear that old coat to day said Mr [Silas] Dean to Dr Franklin on their way to sign the treaty with United States.— "to give it a little revenge. I wore this Coat on the day Wetherburn abused me at Whitehall" said the Doctor.

> Variant of *111* and *204*.

129.   I sat next to Dr Franklin in Congress when he was chosen commissioner to go to France in October 1776. He was then upwards of 70 years of age. Upon my congratulating upon his appointment, he said "I am now like the remnant of a piece of cloath. The Shopkeepers you know generally say when they sell it 'you may have it for what you please.' just so my country may command my Services in any way they chuse."—

> Variant of *80*.

130.   The *Perruquiers* [wigmakers] were at that time a privileged corporation, and it was the policy of the time to preserve their

privileges, rather than have to pay an immense number of pensions, if their privileges were taken away. Franklin, speaking to Turgot on the financial point, observed: "You have in France an excellent source of revenue, may recruit your army at the same time, and it will cost you nothing; let the public refrain from frizzing and powdering their hair; the money saved will be preferable to a tax, and enable the people to pay those that are indispensable; then the *Perruquiers*, being without a vocation, may be embodied in a military corps, the wages of hair-dressing will be saved, and the hair-powder will be converted into provisions."

> M. J. Condorcet, *Vie de Turgot* (1786), trans. William Duane, *Memoirs of BF*, 2 vols. (1834–1840), 1:xxv. The same plan appears in BF's letter, February 1777, with a fine irony: "I wish every Gentleman and Lady in France would only be so obliging as to follow my Fashion, comb their own Heads as I do mine, dismiss their Friseurs, and pay me half the Money they paid to them. You see, the gentry might well afford this, and I could then enlist those Friseurs, who are at least 100,000 and with the Money I would maintain them, make a Visit with them to England, and dress the Heads of your Ministers and Privy Councillors" (Smyth 7:26).

131.   Pass'd the whole of the 29th [of June] in Philadelphia and dined with his Excellency President [of Pennsylvania] Franklin— This dignified Character . . . is now advanced beyond four score and yet seems perfectly in full Exercise of all his mental Abilities— His Perception is quick and Memory very retentive— From Appearances I should suppose him to enjoy uninterrupted Health and great Vigour of Body for his advanced Life— Our Meal was frugal, but his Excellency indulged as to Quantity, drinking only of Beer and very small Russets— We were alone excepting a Daughter (Mrs Beech [Bache]) and two Women from the Country which indulged me with the Opportunity of engrossing him altogether— I found him conversible, communicative *enough,* easy in his Manners and affording all those Attentions which could in Reason be demanded from his Time of Life and Station— He indulged me with the Sight of several Prints executed in Europe, amongst which were General Washington's and that of John Paul Jones— both masterly finished, and was so very obliging as upon my mentioning the Difficulty of procuring a nautical Ephemeris (without knowing him to be possess'd of those Calculations) as to take me to his Library and put into my Hands The *Connaissance de Temps* done in Paris.

> Manuscript diary of Winthrop Sargent, entry for 29 June 1786, Massachusetts Historical Society film, reel 1, frame 115. A thirty-three-year-old Bostonian, Sargent was passing through Philadelphia on his way to survey territory northwest of the Ohio.

132.   While [Gustavus III of Sweden] was in France [June 1784] he was frequently solicited to visit Dr. Franklin, and as often declined. One of the French nobles, who could use a little freedom with the king, begged to know why he denied himself an honour which every other crowned head in Europe would be proud to accept.— "No man," said he, "regards the Doctor's scientific accomplishments more than I do; but the king who affects to like an enthusiast for liberty, is a hypocrite. I love the Doctor as a philosopher, but I hate him as a politician; and nothing shall ever induce me to be in the presence of a man whom my habits and situation obliges me to detest, while it is in my power to avoid it."

> Boston Magazine, 3 (August 1786): 328. Gustavus, a patron of arts and science, had restored absolute monarchy to Sweden. BF's diary for 26 June 1784 records someone asking if he had seen the king: "I had not yet had that Honor" (Smyth 10:347). The anecdote was kept alive in such periodicals as the *Philadelphia Magazine and Review*, 1 (January 1799): 28.

133.   When Dr. Franklin was about twenty years of age, and wrought as a journey-man printer, he took it into his head to live upon bread and water. This regimen, notwithstanding his laborious occupation, he continued for six weeks, eating about a pound of bread a day, and using no other beverage but water, yet he perceived no diminution whatever either in the vigour of his body or his mind. His mother being asked, why her son adopted such a whimsical plan of life, replied, "Because he has read a foolish philosopher called Plutarch; however, I suffer him to take his own way, for I am certain he will soon tire of it."

> *Almanach Littéraire* (Paris) for 1787, rpt., *Pennsylvania Magazine of History and Biography*, 75 (1951): 192; trans. in *Literary and Biographical Magazine*, 6 (April 1791): 25–26. For variant, see 267.

134.   My winter's residence in London was the means of improving my acquaintance with Dr. Franklin. I was seldom many days without seeing him, and being members of the same club, we con-

stantly returned together. . . . The last day that he spent in England, having given out that he should leave London the day before, we passed together, without any other company; and much of the time was employed in reading American newspapers, especially accounts of the reception which the *Boston port bill* met with in America; and as he read the addresses to the inhabitants of Boston from the places in the neighbourhood, the tears trickled down his cheeks.

135.   It is much to be lamented, that a man of Dr. Franklin's general good character, and great influence, should have been an unbeliever in christianity, and also have done so much as he did to make others unbelievers. To me, however, he acknowledged that he had not given so much attention as he ought to have done to the evidences of christianity, and desired me to recommend to him a few treatises on the subject, such as I thought most deserving of his notice, but not of great length, promising to read them, and give me his sentiments on them. Accordingly, I recommended to him Hartley's evidences of christianity in his Observations on Man [which Priestley abridged in 1775], and what I had then written on the subject in my Institutes of natural and revealed religion. But the American war breaking out soon after, I do not believe that he ever found himself sufficiently at leisure for the discussion.

> *Memoirs of Dr. Joseph Priestley*, written 1787 and published in 2 vols. (London, 1806), 1:88–90.

136.   Dr. Franklin lives in Market Street, between Second and Third Streets, but his house stands up a court-yard at some distance from the street. We found him in his Garden, sitting upon a grass plat under a very large Mulberry, with several other gentlemen and two or three ladies. . . . When I entered his house, I felt as if I was going to be introduced to the presence of an European Monarch. But how were my ideas changed, when I saw a short, fat, trunched old man, in a plain Quaker dress, bald pate, and short white locks, sitting without his hat under the tree, and, as Mr. [Elbridge] Gerry introduced me, rose from his chair, took me by the hand, expressed his joy to see me, welcomed me to the city, and begged me to seat myself close to him. His voice was low, but his countenance open, frank, and pleasing. He instantly reminded me of old Captain [John] Cummings, for he is nearly of his pitch, and no more of the air of superiority about him. I delivered him my letters. After he had read them, he

took me again by the hand, and, with the usual compliments, introduced me to the other gentlemen of the company, who were most of
them members of the Convention. Here we entered into a free conversation, and spent our time most agreeably until it was dark. The
tea-table was spread under the tree, and Mrs. Bache, a very gross and
rather homely lady, who is the only daughter of the Doctor and lives
with him, served it out to the company. She had three of her children
about her, over whom she seemed to have no kind of command, but
who appeared to be excessively fond of their Grandpapa.

137.   The Doctor showed me a curiosity he had just received,
and with which he was much pleased. It was a snake with two heads,
preserved in a large vial. . . . The Doctor mentioned the situation of
this snake, if it was traveling among bushes, and one head should
choose to go on one side of the stem of a bush and the other head
should prefer the other side, and that neither of the heads would consent to come back or give way to the other. He was then going to
mention a humorous matter that had that day taken place in Convention, in consequence of his comparing the snake to America, for
he seemed to forget that every thing in Convention was to be kept
a profound secret; but the secrecy of Convention matters was suggested to him, which stopped him, and deprived me of the story he
was going to tell.

For variant, see 65.

138.   After it was dark, we went into the house, and the Doctor
invited me into his library, which is likewise his study. It is a very
large chamber, and high studded. The walls were covered with book-
shelves filled with books; besides, there are four large alcoves, extend-
ing two-thirds of the length of the Chamber, filled in the same
manner. I presume this is the largest, and by far the best, private
library in America. He showed us a glass machine for exhibiting the
circulation of the blood in the arteries and veins of the human body.
. . . Another great curiosity was a rolling press, for taking the copies
of letters or any other writing. A sheet of paper is completely copied
in less than two minutes, the copy as fair as the original, and without
effacing it in the smallest degree. It is an invention of his own, and
extremely useful in many situations in life. He also showed us his
long artificial arm and hand, for taking down and putting books up
on high shelves which are out of reach; and his great armed chair,

with rockers, and a large fan placed over it, with which he fans himself, keeps off flies, etc., while he sits reading, with only a small motion of his foot; and many other curiosities and inventions, all his own, but of lesser note. Over his mantel-tree, he has a prodigious number of medals, busts, and casts in wax or plaster of Paris, which are the effigies of the most noted characters in Europe. But what the Doctor wished principally to show to me was a huge volume on Botany, and which, indeed, afforded me the greatest pleasure of any one thing in his library. It was a single volume, but so large that it was with great difficulty that the Doctor was able to raise it from a low shelf and lift it on to the table; but with that senile ambition common to old people, he insisted on doing it himself, and would permit no person to assist him, merely to show us how much strength he had remaining. It contained the whole of Linnæus Systima Vegetabilia, with large cuts of every plant, and colored from nature. It was a feast to me, and the Doctor seemed to enjoy it as well as myself. We spent a couple of hours in examining this volume, while the other gentlemen amused themselves with other matters.

> In Manasseh Cutler's journal for July 1787 (*Life of Rev. Manasseh Cutler*, ed. W. P. Cutler and J. P. Cutler, 2 vols. [1888], 1:267–270). At forty-five an agent for the fledgling Ohio Company, Cutler was in Philadelphia while Congress drafted the ordinance on administering the new territories.

139.   Most men indeed, as well as most sects in religion, think themselves in possession of all truth, and that wherever others differ from them, it is so far errour. [Richard] Steele, a Protestant, in a dedication, tells the Pope, that the only difference between our two churches, in their opinions of the certainty of their doctrine, is, the Romish church is infallible, and the church of England is *never in the wrong.*

> *Worcester Magazine*, 4 (October 1787):112, giving the text of BF's address to the Constitutional Convention, 17 September. The "Steele" reference is to *Account of the State of the Roman-Catholick Religion* (1715), the Preface of which has a mock dedication to Pope Clement XI ("You are Infallible, and We always in the Right" [p. ii]), signed by Steele but written by Benjamin Hoadly and thus not collected in Steele's works.

140.   But though many private persons, think almost as highly of their own infallibility as that of their Sect— few express it so naturally as a certain French lady, who in a little dispute with her sister, said, I do not know how it happens, sister, but I meet with no body but myself that is always in the right.

> *Ibid.* This story was taken to be factual: "The duchess de la Ferté remarked one day to mademoiselle de Launay, who later became madame de Staël: 'The truth is, my dear daughter, that I am the only one who is always right'" (Philip Mazzei, *Researches on the United States* [1788], trans. C. D. Sherman [1976], p. 400n).

141.   I shall close with an account of the Polly Baker story, which the abbé [Raynal] claims to be true. "Laws are still too severe in these areas [of America]. Their rigor can be gauged from the speech of a girl made recently to the magistrates when she was convicted for bearing her fifth illegitimate child." Polly Baker's speech produced, he said, "an astonishing revolution in New England. The court did not punish her, she was not even fined, and as a final triumph, she married one of her judges."

One day at the close of 1777 or early in 1778 the abbé called on Dr. Franklin and found Mr. [Silas] Deane with him. "We were speaking of your book," said Mr. Deane, "and saying you were poorly informed about America, especially about New England." As the abbé wished to argue the point, Mr. Deane quoted several passages in which there was not a word of truth. They then discussed the Polly Baker anecdote and here the debate grew more serious, because the abbé insisted he had found the story in an authentic report. After some time Dr. Franklin spoke: "Sir, I am going to give you the facts. When I was young at times I lacked materials to fill the pages of my gazette, so I amused myself by writing stories and the yarn about Polly Baker is one of them." "Well," replied the abbé, "I prefer to have your stories in my book than truth from many other people."

> Philip Mazzei, *Researches in the United States* (1788), trans. C. D. Sherman (1976), pp 214–215. Raynal treated Polly Baker as fact in his *Histoire . . . les Deux-Indes* (1770), bk. 17. For variant, see 250.

142.   Dr. F. being in England in the year 1775, was asked by a Nobleman, what would satisfy the Americans? He answered, that it

might easily be comprised in a few Re's, which he immediately wrote
on a piece of paper. Thus

Re: {
-call your forces,
-store Castle William,
-pair the damage done to Boston,
-peal your unconstitutional acts,
-nounce your pretensions to taxes,
-fund the duties you have extorted; after this
-quire, and
-ceive payment for the destroyed tea, with the vol-
   untary grants of the colonies, and then
-joice in a happy
-conciliation.

> *American Magazine* (New York), 1 (March 1788): 247; a favorite
> of the jestbooks in the nineties—e.g., *Funny Stories* (1795), p. 8,
> and *American Jestbook* (1796), p. 10.

143.   After the news of the destruction of the stamped paper
had arrived in England, the ministry again sent for the doctor, to
consult with him, and concluded with this proposition, that if the
Americans would engage to pay for the damage done in the destruction of the stamped paper, etc. the parliament would then repeal the
act. To this the doctor answered, that it put him in mind of a Frenchman, who having heated a poker red hot, ran into the street, and
addressing an Englishman he met there, "Ha, monsieur, voulez-vous
givé me de plaisir et de satisfaction, and leté me runi dis poker one
foote up your backside?" "What!" says the Englishman:— "Only to
leté me runi dis poker only one foote up your backside." "Damn your
soul," replies the Englishman. "Welle, den, only so far," says the
Frenchman, pointing to about six inches of the poker.— "No, no,"
replies the Englishman, "damn your soul; what do you mean?" "Well,
den," says the Frenchman, "will you havé de justice to payé me for
de trouble and expence of heating de poker?"— "No, damn me, if I
do," answered the Englishman, and walked off.

> *American Museum*, 4 (August 1788): 184. This is the variant of
> 16 that caused his sister to chide BF about such language as
> "damn your soul," which of course was not in his own version,
> as he explained in 57. Some periodicals printed "D——n"—*Massa-
> chusetts Centinel*, 1 November 1788—while jestbooks preferred the
> unexpurgated "Damn"—for example, *Funny Stories* (1795) pp.
> 23-24.

144.   The day on which the federal convention agreed to the new constitution, presented to the public, the great Dr. Franklin asked a gentleman who sat next to him, whether he had taken notice of the picture of the sun in the recess at the back of the president's chair? He replied that he had, but not with a particular attention. The doctor then observed that painters had been puzzled to paint a single sun in such manner that the spectator could determine whether it was a rising or a setting sun; he added, that he had viewed the picture before mentioned as often as he had been in the hall, and never had been able to come to a determination, but *now* he was sure it was a *rising sun*.

> *American Jest Book* (1789), p. 18. For James Madison's version, see *274*.

145.   While doctor *Franklin* was at Paris last war, he happened to mention at his table, that he had but little Madeira wine; upon which an American guest [Peter Allaire] sent him three dozen. A few days afterwards, this gentleman was thrown into the Bastile, and confined there several weeks, without the least intimation of what he was accused of; only on his earnest enquiry, one of the officers told him he was afraid it would go hard with him, and asked him whether he was a catholic, and would be attended by a priest, which he, being a protestant, refused. After some time, a bottle of wine was brought, and he was asked whether he knew what wine it was, and was ordered to drink it: he complied, and answered that he believed it was some of his own Madeira. At length he was released, and then he discovered that doctor Franklin had been taken ill, soon after he received his present, and it was imagined that he had been hired by the English Court to poison the doctor.

> Ibid., pp. 11–12. The guest was identified by Bernard Faÿ, F, *the Apostle of Modern Times* (1929), p. 450.

146.   The late Frederic [King of Prussia] was fully sensible of the contagious nature of liberty. He knew that the spirit of freedom was epidemical, and he did not choose to employ his subjects in any mode that could put them in the way of catching the disorder. When dr. Franklin applied to him, to lend his assistance to America, "Pray, doctor," says the veteran, "what is the object they mean to attain?" "Liberty, sire," replied the philosopher, "liberty—that freedom which is the birth right of man."— The king, after a short pause, made this

memorable answer:— "I was born a prince; I am become a king, and I will not use the power which I possess, to the ruin of my own trade. I was born to command—and the people are born to obey."

> *American Museum*, 6 (November 1789): 411. The French jestbook, *Frankliniana* (1818) reprinted this without the last sentence (p. 36); thereafter, the shortened version appeared in such collections as the *Percy Anecdotes*, 2 vols. (1834), 2:103.

147.   When the President of the United States, in his late tour, was at Lexington, viewing the field where the first blood was shed in the later war; he with a degree of good humour, told his informant, and others that were present, that the Britons complained to Dr. Franklin of the ill usage their troops met with at Lexington battle, by the Yankies getting behind the stone walls, and firing at them; the Doctor replied, by asking them *whether there were not two sides to the wall.*

> *Gazette of the United States*, 16 December 1789, probably from the *Boston Semi-Weekly Advertiser*, 27 November 1789, reporting details of Washington's tour through the Lexington-Watertown area on 5 November.

148.   When I was in Philadelphia attending the federal convention June 1787, I waited on Dr. Franklin one morning to pay my respects to him and after some little conversation which was of a gay and cheerful kind he gave me an opportunity to ask him his age, when he informed me he was 82 years old, to which he observed that he had "lived long enough to intrude himself on posterity."

> Journal of William Leigh Pierce, *Journal of American History*, 1 (1907): 703. This entry was not included in Pierce's "Characters in the Convention," with its better-known description of BF as not shining much in public and telling a story "in a style more engaging than anything I ever heard" (*American Historical Review*, 3 [1898]: 328).

149.   I have omitted the greatest indignity that was ever offered to me. Soon after my return from Virginia I called on the Doctor, and shewed him Mr. [Patrick] Henry's Certificate, and requested his patronage in promoteing a subscription to compleat my great undertakeing. Altho he had said everything in favour of the scheme that he could, he refused to give me a certificate of the sort, or even to

put his name to a subscription paper, but called me into another room, opened his desk and took out 5 or Six Dollars, and offered them to me. The Indignation which inflamed my Blood could hardly be suppressed. Yet [I] refused it with all the Modisty that I was master of, and informed him that I could not receive money unless it was moneys that should be subscribed for, was I to do that I laid myself liable to censure of imbezzling monies that was given for other purposes. I esteem that one of the most imprudent acts of my life, that I had not treated that insult with the indignity which he merited, and stomped the paltry ore under my feet.

> Autobiography of John Fitch, ed. F. D. Prager (1976), p. 166. Fitch had sought BF's help in September-October 1785 for financing construction of a steamboat.

150.   His conversation with his family upon the subject of his dissolution was free and cheerful. A few days before he died, he rose from his bed and begged that it might be made up for him so that he might die "in a decent manner." His daughter told him that she hoped he would recover and live many years longer. He calmly replied, "He hoped not." Upon being advised to change his position in bed that he might breathe *easy*, he said "A dying man can do nothing *easy*."

> Letter from Benjamin Rush to Dr. Richard Price, one of BF's dearest friends in England, 24 April 1790, ed. L. H. Butterfield, *Letters of Benjamin Rush*, 1:564. Without the last sentence, this was made part of BF's obituary in the *Gentleman's Magazine* for June 1790 (60:573) and subsequently widely reprinted.

151.   Dr. Franklin, when a child, found the long graces used by his father before and after meals very disagreeable. One day after the winter's provisions had been salted, "I think, father," says Benjamin, "if you said *grace* over the *whole cask*—once for all—it would be a vast *saving of time*."

> *American Museum*, 7 (May 1790): 228. This was reprinted in an early biography by Alexander Stephens, *Private Life of the Late BF* (1793) as an example of young BF's lighthearted attitude toward "Puritanism" (p. 195): see the consequence of this view in variant 263.

152.   I never shall forget one day that I passed with our friend last summer. I found him in bed in great agony, but when that agony abated a little, I asked if I should read to him; he said, Yes; and the first book I met with was Johnson's Lives of the Poets. I read the life of [Isaac] Watts, who was a favourite author with Dr. F.; and, instead of lulling him to sleep, it roused him to a display of the powers of his memory and his reason: he repeated several of Watts's Lyric Poems, and descanted upon their sublimity in a strain worthy of them and of their pious author.

> Letter by Mary Hewson, the former Mary Stevenson of 10, to Thomas Viny, 5 May 1790, rpt., the Monthly Repository, 16 (1821): 4.

153.   A certain English Philosopher [Benjamin Wilson] pretended in opposition to dr. Franklin, that blunt conductors were the only safe ones. The king of Great Britain, during the war, changed the sharp conductors of his palace into blunt ones as though he disdained to owe his safety to an enemy's invention. This he persisted in, notwithstanding the Royal Society's public condemnation of the pretended improvement. This anecdote caused the following epigram:

> While you, great George, for safety hunt,
> And sharp conductors change for blunt,
>   The nation's out of joint.
> Franklin a wiser course pursues:
> And all your thunder, fearless views,
>   By keeping to the point.

> American Museum, 7 (June 1790): 344. The controversy about blunt versus pointed lightning rods raged in 1772, but George III ordered the change to blunt rods in 1777. The anecdote and epigram were kept alive in jestbooks like Joke Upon Joke (1818), p. 64, and collections like Alexander Garden, Anecdotes of the Revolutionary War (1822), p. 411.

154.   Of his origin he made no secret. In a conversation at Paris, in company with the Comte d'Aranda and the Duke de la Rochefoucault, he replied to an Irish gentleman, who had asked him some questions about the state of the paper-manufactory there, "Few men can give you more information on that subject than myself, for I was originally in the printing trade."

155.   At every entertainment which he gave his workmen,
during the life of [John] Watts, the health of his old friend and master
was one of the first toasts; and he used to relate several pleasant anecdotes of him: for Watts, with much good sense, and not a small share
of pointed wit or something extremely like it, had a *manner* of saying
and doing things, that was exclusively his own. . . . He soon discovered in him that vigour of intellect which has been since universally
acknowledged; and often affirmed, with an oath, that his "young
American *composer*," as he called him, would one day make a considerable figure in the world.

> Obituary in the *Gentleman's Magazine*, 60 (June 1790): 571, con-
> ceivably written by the editor, David Henry, who had worked
> with BF at Watts's shop and remained a lifelong friend.

156.   When he came to Philadelphia in 1723, he was first employed by one [Samuel] Keimer, a printer,— a visionary whose mind
was frequently elevated above the little concerns of life, and consequently very subject to mistakes, which he seldom took the pains
to correct. Franklin had frequently reasoned with him upon the importance of accuracy in his profession, but in vain. His fertile head
however soon furnished him with an opportunity to second his argu-
ments by proof. They soon after undertook the impression of a primer,
which had been lately published in New-England. Franklin overlooked the piece; and when his master had set the following couplet—

> When the last trumpet soundeth,
>   We shall not all die:
> But we shall all be *changed*
>   In the twinkling of an eye,

he privately removed the letter *c*, and it was printed off—

> When the last trumpet soundeth,
>   We shall not all die:
> But we shall all be *hanged*
>   In the twinkling of an eye.

> *American Museum*, 8 (July 1790): 24. BF had used the example
> of changing "changed" to "hanged" in the *Pennsylvania Gazette*,
> 13 March 1730 (see *1*), and *Poor Richard's Almanac* for 1750
> (P 1:169; 3:438)—but with no allusion to Keimer.

The next ten anecdotes are translated from André Morellet, "Anecdotes sur Francklin," *Gazette Nationale, ou Le Moniteur Universel,* 15 July 1790, p. 805.

157.   One day Francklin demonstrated for a credulous man the experiment of calming waves on a pond with oil, and to enhance the performance acted with exaggerated gravity. Duly impressed, the man asked: "But what, sir, should I derive from all this?" *"Nothing,"* said Francklin, "but what you see."

158.   At Philadelphia, an Indian came to watch Francklin perform the experiment of igniting brandy with an electric spark: "These White-men are very clever rascals" says he, without showing the least surprise or the slightest reflection.

159.   This celebrated figure would sometimes tell about the days when he was a Philadelphia printer. One of his Journeymen, a good worker, would never come to work before Wednesdays, so the philosophical Printer took him aside: "Francis, you do not think ahead. If you worked more constantly now, you could be putting something aside that would buy you leisure in your old age." "I have it all figured out," says the Journeyman. "I have an uncle, a Druggist in Cheapside (a district in London), and he planned to work for twenty years till he earned £4000 so he could then live like a Gentleman. He was going to make himself a Gentleman by wholesale. Me, I would rather do it by retail, and do nothing at all half each week for the next twenty years than do nothing at all the whole week twenty years from now."

160.   After the declaration of independence, when each American State busily drafted new laws and set up a form of Government to replace the old forms, the Pennsylvania Assembly held many great debates. But at the end of two or three months they found themselves not much further along than when they had started. Still, everything in the state had been going on smoothly, with no trouble or public unrest. One day Francklin says to the Delegates: "Gentlemen, you see we have been living under Anarchy and yet the business of living has gone on as usual. Be careful. If our debates go on too much longer, the people may come to see it is possible to get along without us very well."

161.   Francklin would use the next Anecdote to illustrate how one could correct flaws in his character with time and patience. "One day," says he, "I was in a Smith's shop when a man came in to buy an axe. When the Smith sharpened axes, he would leave them unburnished, but this customer wanted one polished brightly. The Smith told him it would take a long time to do that, and he would need someone to turn the grindstone. The customer offered to turn it himself, and so the two of them set to work. After a little while, our man wants to see how the polishing is coming along. He sees very little progress. He returns to the wheel, coming back from time to time, and seeing only a few shiny spots. Finally, tired of turning, he says to the Smith: 'Honest, I do not really mind if it is no more polished than that. I will buy it as it is.' Thus, Francklin would say, "we become accustomed to our faults. We quickly quit turning the grindstone that would correct them. But, I would add, if the axe cuts well enough, it does not need to be burnished."

> This is a variant of BF's anecdote in the *Autobiography*; see *50*.

162.   One day, wishing to tour the Factories at Norwich, he was guided through the shops by a big Manufacturer who told him: "These cloths are for Italy, those for Germany, the ones over there for the American islands, and those for the Continent." While he listened, Francklin noticed that the Workers were half-naked or in tatters, and, turning to his guide, he asks: "have you none for the Factory-Workers of Norwich?"

163.   After the peace of 1783, when talking of corruption in the English Parliament, Francklin would say that if, before the war, the United States had given him one-quarter of what the war had cost them, he would have guaranteed to buy their independence from England at that price.

> This is a variant of Benjamin Rush's version—see *124*—where the figure is "one-tenth" rather than "one-quarter."

164.   Removed from his Office of Post-Master of New-York by the King of England, Francklin returned to America. War was declared, and the King of England lost America and the Post Office revenue. Francklin would say: "Since I lost my office, I have not earned a thing from it, but neither has the King."

This echoes the *Autobiography*, as BF, speaking of being dismissed from his post as deputy postmaster general of North America, says: "We had brought it to yield *three times* as much clear Revenue to the Crown as the Post-Office of Ireland. Since that imprudent Transaction, they have receiv'd from it,— Not one Farthing" (NCE p. 389).

165.   Francklin attended one cultural Event where there was many a speech. He understood very little of French oratory, yet, wishing to be polite, he decided to applaud whenever he saw his friend, Madame de Boufflers, make any sign of satisfaction. After the meeting, his grandson exclaimed: "But, papa, you were applauding whenever they praised you, and much louder than anyone else." He would tell of his embarrassment and the obvious—that there was simply no way to get out of it.

166.   Lord Shelburne, now Lansdowne [Sir William Petty], says that in his dealings with Francklin, he noticed that his primary trait was never to trouble himself about forcing events but to profit well from those which came about—that he had the "medicine expectative."

167.   In private life this philosopher was not exempted from the little imperfections and weaknesses of human nature: irregular in his addresses to the Cyprian goddess [Aphrodite], the legal partner of his bed complained of infidelities. It is well known, he had mistresses plenty; and there are several living testimonies of his licentious amours.— A gentleman of Philadelphia, who was very intimate with him, has frequently told the following anecdote: that walking some years since in an afternoon, near the doctor's house, he perceived a quarrel between two females before his door. On approaching nearer, he found that one of them was the doctor's housekeeper, and the other a comely washerwoman, who had been also honoured with his intimate acquaintance: the one was in place, the other *cashiered*; and therefore it could be no wonder they had no great esteem for each other. The contest was sharp both in words and blows; the streets re-echoed with their shrieks, and their caps flew in pieces; while the Doctor, from a window, beheld the battle, and laughed most heartily.— *Nemo mortalium omnibus horis sapit* [No man is wise all the time]; and philosophers have their frailties like other men.

[?Andrew Allen and James Jones Wilmer,] *Memoirs of the Late Dr. Benjamin Franklin* (1790), pp. 91-92. On the authorship of this scurrilous biography, see my note in *Early American Literature*, 10 (1975): 220–221. This anecdote seems concocted from two earlier attacks, both politically motivated: In a pamphlet of 1764, *What is Sauce for a Goose*, BF is said to have employed as a kitchen wench and prostitute a maid named Barbara; and in the *Morning Post* of 1 June 1779, he is said to have fathered his son William "by an oyster wench in Philadelphia, whom he left to die in the streets of disease and hunger," echoed also in 89.

168.　　When the Doctor first heard of the French Revolution, it was in the company of several persons who came to visit him at Philadelphia, when he could no longer go abroad; every one was wondering at the circumstance, and asking whether it was not very singular. The Doctor having heard them for some time, with his usual patience, at last replied— "Why I see nothing singular in all this, but, on the contrary, what might naturally be expected; the French have served an *apprenticeship* to *Liberty* in this country, and now that they are out of their time, they *have set up for themselves.*"

> *Gazette of the United States*, 4 September 1790, p. 583; *American Museum*, 9 (February 1791): 116.

169.　　The American philosopher presented his grandson to Voltaire, with a request that he would give him his benediction. "God and liberty!" said Voltaire: "it is the only benediction which can be given to the grandson of Franklin." They went together to a public assembly of the academy of sciences, and the public at the same time beheld with emotion these two men. . . . They embraced each other in the midst of public acclamations, and it was said to be Solon who embraced Sophocles.

> M. J. Condorcet, *Life of Voltaire*, 2 vols. (London, 1790), 1:423–424. For variants, see 89 and 201.

170.　　The succession to Dr. Franklin at the court of France, was an excellent school of humility. On being presented to any one as the Minister of America, the common-place question, used in such cases, was 'c'est vous, Monsieur, qui remplace le Docteur Franklin?' 'It is you, Sir, who replace Doctor Franklin?' I generally answered 'no one can replace him, Sir; I am only his successor."

> Letter by Thomas Jefferson to William Smith, who was seeking

materials for a eulogy of BF, 1 March 1791, ed. J. P. Boyd,
Papers of TJ, 19:113; William Smith, *Eulogium on BF* (1792), p. 33.

171.   While the Doctor resided in France as minister from
America during the war, he had numerous proposals made to him
by projectors of every country and of every kind, who wished to go
to the land that floweth with milk and honey, America; and among
the rest, there was one who offered himself to the King. He introduced
his proposal to the Doctor by letter, which is now in the hands of
M. [Caron de] Beaumarchais, of Paris— stating, first, that as the
Americans had dismissed or sent away their King, that they would
want another. Secondly, that himself was a Norman. Thirdly, that
he was of a more ancient family than the Dukes of Normandy, and
of a more honourable descent, his line having never been bastardized.
Fourthly, that there was already a precedent in England, of Kings
coming out of Normandy: and on these grounds he rested his offer,
enjoining that the Doctor would forward it to America. But as the
Doctor did not do this, nor yet send him an answer, the projector
wrote a second letter; in which he did not, it is true, threaten to go
over and conquer America, but only, with great dignity, proposed,
that if his offer was not accepted, that an acknowledgment of about
£30,000 might be made to him for his generosity!

> Thomas Paine, *Rights of Man* (1791), as "an anecdote which I
> had from Dr. Franklin," p. 65.

172.   While he was President of the State of Pennsylvania, the
Doans, it may be remembered, were tried, condemned and executed.—
A religious madman called upon the President, and asserted that he
was sent to command him to grant a reprieve to those unfortunate
young men.— "Who sent you?" "The Lord." "You are an impostor,"
replied Dr. Franklin— "The Lord could not have sent you on so silly
an errand;— *they were hanged two hours ago.*"

> *Federal Gazette*, 15 April 1791. The Doane cousins, Levi and
> Abraham, were executed 24 September 1788, after six years of
> banditry—despite public appeals for their reprieve.

173.   Doctor Franklin, being in France previous to the revolution, when the true spirit of gallantry was fashionable, and before
it had been superseded by the fire of patriotism, and an itch for

political liberty, our American received frequent attentions from the most celebrated beauties and those the most remarkable for wit, elegance, and politeness, in the French metropolis. A lady of this description, who, being a favourite, was particularly pleased with the old gentleman's company, was one day sitting on his knee and combing his grey locks:— "Why," asked he, "have you, that have so often invited me to dine and sup with you, never requested me to stay and sleep." She smiled— perhaps she blushed— and answered, "she would be happy to be favoured with his company that very night."— Fortunately it was summer time.— "Hum, hum," said the old gentleman, a little embarrassed, not expecting so warm a reply, but taking out a memorandum book, *"I'll make a minute of the invitation, and when the nights are longer, will have the pleasure of waiting on you."*

> *American Museum,* 10 (October 1791):176, and widely reprinted (e.g., *Beers' Almanac* [Hartford, Ct., 1799]) even as late as 1928 (Bernard Faÿ, "Last Loves of the First American," *The Forum,* 79:330).

174.   In [the Athenian Club], it was once observed that the members in general, though very good men, much beloved by their friends, and some of them much admired by the public, were under the imputation of irreligion, because they never went to church.

Dr. Franklin, who was expected to be jocose on the subject, took it up seriously; and said, though he could not rescue his character, by attending the long tedious services of the church, yet he never passed a place of public worship on a Sunday, without feeling some regret, that he had not an opportunity of joining in a rational form of devotion. All the members expressed similar sentiments; and Mr. [David] Williams was requested to draw up a form [liturgy] for the consideration of such members of the club as wished to join in the undertaking. . . . Just at the termination of this business, Dr. Franklin was obliged suddenly to quit England; and the American war broke out. The associated philosophers were frightened, and declined pursuing a plan, in which the unpopular name of Franklin might be mentioned.

> Thomas Morris, *A General View of the Life and Writings of the Rev. David Williams* (1792), pp. 11–12. Williams's autobiography says an eminent lawyer, James Adair, inspired him to prepare his rational liturgy, published in 1774 as *A Liturgy on the Principles of the Christian Religion* (David Williams, "Bibliography of

David Williams," *National Library of Wales Journal,* 10 [1957]: 126–127).

175.   In the summer of 1766 . . . I once had a curious conversation with Franklin at the table, when he dined with me. We talked much about America, about the savages, the rapid growth of the English colonies, the growth of the population, its duplication in twenty-five years, etc. I said that when I was in London in 1741 I might have learned more about the condition of the Colonies by English books and pamphlets, had I then thought seriously of what I had even then expressed to others, that they would one day release themselves from England. People laughed at me, but still I believed it. He answered me with his earnest and expressive face: "Then you were mistaken. The Americans have too much love for their mother country." I said, "I believe it, but almighty interest would soon outweigh that love or extinguish it altogether." He could not deny that this was possible, but secession was impossible, for all the American towns of importance, Boston, New York, and Philadelphia, could be destroyed by bombardment. This was unanswerable.

> Autobiography of Johann D. Michaelis, professor of theology of Göttingen, trans., J. G. Rosengarten, "F's Visit to Germany," *Proceedings of the Pennsylvania-German Society,* 13 (1904): 52–53.

176.   The celebrated Dr. Franklin sent word, one christmas morning, to some of his literary friends that he intended to kill a turkey for their entertainment by a discharge of one of his electrical batteries, and that the process of cooking might be carried on equally as philosophical, he intended to have it roasted by a fire kindled with the electrical fluid. He began the business of charging his bottles, but before he had quite completed the process, by some casualty the whole battery was discharged through his own body. He was so violently stunned by this misfortune that he lay, a considerable length of time, in a state of insensibility. Shortly after the Doctor had recovered his senses, some of his friends coming into the room enquired what was the matter! Ah, gentlemen, replied he, I informed you of my intention to kill a turkey by electricity, but, alas, my design miscarried and I had like to have killed a *goose.*

> *Feast of Merriment; a New American Jester* (1795), p. 12. The factual basis of the story, but not the punch line, is in BF's letter of 25 December 1750 (P 4:82–83). For variant, see *304.*

177.   The sagacious Dr. Franklin used to say, that the purest and most useful friend a man could possibly procure, was a French-woman of a certain age who had no designs upon his person; "they are," added he, "so ready to do you service, and from their knowledge of the world know so well how to serve you wisely."

> William Seward, *Anecdotes of Some Distinguished Persons*, 3d ed., 3 vols. (1796), 3:345n.

178.   When Franklin was on his mission to France previous to the alliance, he put up one night at an inn near the frontiers. Gibbon, the celebrated historian, happening to be in the same house, Franklin sent his compliments, requesting the pleasure of spending the evening with Gibbon. In answer he received a card, importing, that "notwithstanding Mr. Gibbon's regard for the character of Dr. Franklin, as a man and a philosopher, he could not reconcile it with his duty to his King, to have any conversation with a *revolted subject*!" Franklin in reply wrote a note, declaring that "though Mr. Gibbon's principles had compelled him to withhold the pleasure of his conversation, Dr. Franklin still had such a respect for the character of Mr. Gibbon, as a gentleman and a historian, that when, in the course of his writing the history of the *decline and fall* of empires, the *decline and fall* of the British empire should come to be his subject, as he expected it soon would, Dr. Franklin would be happy to furnish him with *ample materials* which were in his possession."

> William Cobbett quoting from "the New-York Daily Advertiser" in *Peter Porcupine's Gazette*, 18 October 1797, rpt., *Works*, 12 vols. (1801), 7:244–245. The story was current much earlier, for Horace Walpole alludes to it in a letter of 25 April 1781, speaking of BF as a true politician, "when he said he would furnish Mr Gibbon with materials for writing the History of the Decline of the British Empire" (*Correspondence with William Mason*, eds. W. S. Lewis, et al., 2 vols. [1955], 2:135).

179.   The doctor, in early life, was economical from principle; in his latter days, perhaps from habit. Poor Richard held the purse strings of the president of Pennsylvania. Permit me to illustrate this observation, by an anecdote. Soon after I was introduced, an airy, thoughtless relation, from a New England state, entered the room. It seems he was on a party of pleasure, and had been so much involved

in it, for three weeks, as not to have paid his respects to his venerable relative. The purpose of his present visit was, to solicit the loan of a small sum of money, to enable him to pay his bills, and transport himself home. He preluded his request, with a detail of embarrassments, which might have befallen the most circumspect. He said that he had loaded a vessel for B——, and as he did not deal on credit, had purchased beyond his current cash, and could not readily procure a draft upon home. The doctor, inquiring how much he wanted, he replied, with some hesitation, fifty dollars. The benevolent old gentleman went to his escritoir, and counted him out an hundred. He received them with many promises of punctual payment, and hastily took up the writing implements, to draught a note of hand, for the cash. The doctor, who saw into the nature of the borrower's embarrassments, better than he was aware; and was possessed with the improbability of ever recovering his cash again, stepped across the room, laying his hand gently upon his cousin's arm, said, stop cousin, we will save the paper; a quarter of a sheet is not of great value, but it is worth saving: conveying, at once, a liberal gift and gentle reprimand for the borrower's prevarication and extravagance.

180.   Since I am talking of Franklin, the reader may be as unwilling to leave him as I was. Allow me to relate another anecdote. I do not recollect how the conversation was introduced; but a young person in company, mentioned his surprize, that the possession of great riches should ever be attended with such anxiety and solicitude; and instanced Mr. R—— M——, who, he said, though in possession of unbounded wealth, yet was as busy and more anxious, than the most assiduous clerk in his counting house. The Doctor took an apple from a fruit basket, and presented it to a little child, who could just totter about the room. The child could scarce grasp it in his hand. He then gave it another, which occupied the other hand. Then choosing a third, remarkable for its size and beauty, he presented that also. The child, after many ineffectual attempts to hold the three, dropped the last on the carpet, and burst into tears. See there, said the philosopher; there is a little man, with more riches than he can enjoy.

> Royall Tyler, *The Algerine Captive*, 2 vols. (Walpole, N.H., 1797), 1:155–158. This is a bit more than half of Chapter XXIII, in which the hero-narrator calls on BF to pick up documents to be delivered as he journeys southward.

181.   When the Doctor first arrived at Paris, as Minister Pleni-potentiary of the United States, he intended to conform to the eti-quette of the Court of Versailles, in the article of dress, and accordingly began with sending to a perruquier to make him a wig. On the appointed day, this artificial covering for the head was brought home and tried on; but no attempts of the artist, although he had employed one of the first in Paris, were able to get the wig on his head.

The Doctor, after patiently submitting, for a long time, to the unavailing efforts of the perruquier, at length ventured to give it as his opinion that the wig was too little. This assertion was stoutly denied; but, after very many fruitless trials, the barber threw it down in a passion, exclaiming, "No, Sir, the wig is not too small; but your head is too large."

> *Weekly Magazine*, 1 (3 March 1798): 142–143. BF's sometime secretary, John Vaughan, is said to have told this story as fact in Joshua Francis Fisher, *Recollections* (1929), p. 526.

182.   I set out for Paris with letters of introduction from Dr. Franklin, to several of his philosophical friends. When I parted with the Doctor, he asked me "how I was provided with money for my jaunt." I told him I believed I had enough. "Perhaps not, you may be exposed to unexpected expenses. Here, said he, is a credit upon a Banker in Paris for two or three hundred guineas." I thankfully ac-cepted his kind and generous offer. . . . A day or two after I arrived in London I called upon Dr. Franklin, and informed him . . . that I had been obliged to avail myself of his kind offer, by drawing upon his Banker for 30 guineas. He seemed pleased and requested that I would pay them when convenient to his wife in Philadelphia. This I did, out of the first money I earned after my arrival. Mrs. Franklin for a while refused to receive it for the Doctor had not mentioned the debt to her in any of his letters.

> Benjamin Rush, *Autobiography*, ed. G. W. Corner (1948), pp. 66, 74.

The next eleven anecdotes are translated from papers of BF's close friend at Passy, Abbé Lefebvre de la Roche, rpt., Gilbert Chinard, "Abbé Lefebvre de la Roche's Rec-ollections of BF," *Proceedings of the American Philosophical Society*, 94 (1950): 218–221.

183.   As minister plenipotentiary in his old age, he got along with only one servant. He said that with two you had but half of one, and with three, hardly any at all.

184.   When he was in London, a member of the House of Lords took him to see a house he had just built in a narrow street on land that was so irregular all the rooms had to be oddly shaped and inconveniently arranged. The beautiful columns decorating the front made the rest of the house seem smaller. "My lord," Franklin told him, "if you wish to enjoy your house and its superb colonnade more, all you need do is rent a spacious apartment directly across the street."

185.   In numerous company, he would say little but sit there listening earnestly to the conversation. When friends asked why, he would explain: "If you Frenchmen talked a quarter as much, I could understand it and not have to leave good company so often not knowing what they had talked about."

186.   A nephew of some friends visited Franklin and mentioned that he wished an uncle would give him some useless piece of furniture. The Philosopher told him about a Quaker acquaintance who invited him to see a house he had just built. "I was struck immediately by the grandeur of the place, since the Quaker lived alone and rarely entertained. I asked him, 'Why do you need such huge rooms? You live here alone with only a servant.' 'It's nothing. I can afford it.' At each piece of furniture and each ornament, the same question and always the same answer. Finally, I saw in the vast dining room a beautiful, grand mahogany table easily capable of seating 25 people. 'Why do you need such a grand table?' Once again he replied, 'It's nothing. I can afford it.' But this time I told him, 'Why don't you have a hat that size? You can afford it.' "

187.   All kinds of adventurers would come to him asking for letters of recommendation to Americans. "What good would such letters be," he would say, "when I know you no better than the people do to whom I would recommend you?" He very much admired one letter from a lady at Court who recommended a close relative in these words: "Sir, if you have people in America who know how to reform an awful youth who has been making his family miserable, I beg you to send to them the bearer of this letter. You will thereby perform a miracle worthy of you and oblige yours, etc." The youth did go to America, where he died bravely under fire.

188.   The former Queen of France was amazed to find so much genius behind so modest an exterior and such genuine simplicity amidst the opulent ministers of the great European powers. One day she asked a Courtier what Franklin had been before he became an ambassador. "Foreman of a printshop," said he. "That's so," said another with more sense: "In France he would have become no more than a Bookseller."

189.   With the Peace concluded and America's liberty thus assured, Franklin made ready to return to his Homeland, even though suffering from a cruel illness that made his friends fear he could not survive the rigors of a long sea voyage. The Widow d'Helvétius, who loved him dearly, pressed him to remain in France where he could be attended by skilled physicians, then spend the rest of his days with her and the friends who loved him.

But Jefferson, his friend and successor in France, said: "If I have the misfortune of seeing this great man remain here and die, I would have no alternative but, for the good of our country, to carry him back in his coffin, convinced as I am that the mere presence of his corpse would help to consolidate our revolution."

190.   Thus, despite pleas for him to remain, the man who had already braved so many dangers for his nation and the cause of liberty, stood firm in his resolve to return home and sacrifice what life he still had. "Do not," he told his friends, "do not make my leaving sadder still. Do not add to my sorrow. Help me sustain the spirit I need to leave. My task is unfinished. The little life I still have I owe to those who have trusted me with theirs. I am ill, it is true, but nature, which has treated me so kindly before, will surely allow me the time to answer my countrymen's call. If I do survive after doing my duty to my country, my greatest happiness will be to end my days in the land where I enjoyed so many pleasures among the most enlightened men of Europe."

191.   Age had done nothing to make his soul less sensitive. Walking one day with a friend in the Bois de Boulogne, he spoke of his child who had died aged seven, 40 years earlier: "I still grieve from that loss so long ago. Alas, I will always imagine this son would have been the best of my children."

192.   Of the deceased friends of Madame Helvetius, the person of whom she spoke with most attachment, next to her husband, was Dr. Franklin, who had been almost an inmate of her house when

living at Passy, in the neighbourhood. Rallying her one day on her passion for Helvetius, the Doctor told her that he, as well as herself, had cause to complain of his inconstancy. "In my dreams last night," says the Doctor, "I found that your husband and my wife had met by accident in Paradise, and were married together. I have reason, Madam, to be as angry at this incident as you; but as there is no remedy, *vengeons nous.*" Madame Helvetius, however, it seems, had no faith in dreams.

> Helen Maria Williams, *Sketches of the State of Manners and Opinions in the French Republic*, 2 vols. (1801), 2:223, echoing the bagatelle now known as "The Elysian Dream," written in 1778 and published in the French edition of BF's works in 1798.

193.   The Doctor's mother, it seems, went to church in the forenoon, became his mother in the intermission, and the infant was baptized in the afternoon,— so that the Doctor used humorously to say that he attended meeting the whole of that day.

> Letter by Benjamin Silliman, Yale's first chemistry professor, talking about family traditions, 22 May 1801, in *Life of Benjamin Silliman*, ed. G. P. Fisher, 2 vols. (1866), 1:73. BF was in fact baptized on the day he was born. (*P* 1:3).

 The next four anecdotes are from entries made in 1801 in *Diaries of Sylvester Douglas, Lord Glenbervie*, son-in-law of Lord North, ed. Francis Bickley, 2 vols. (1928), 1:285–287.

194.   [George Hammond our Minister in America], who had been secretary with David Hartley when he went to Paris to settle the Commercial Treaty in 1783, and had frequent occasion of seeing and knowing Franklin, thought to obtain favour on his arrival in America [in 1791] by mentioning that circumstance. But he found that it was far from a popular topic. Franklin had died two or three years before, and his memory was universally detested. [John] Adams, [John] Jay, and [Rufus] King, etc. hated him. He died very rich (a daughter to whom he left the bulk of his fortune and with whom he was said to have an incestuous intercourse, having acknowledged that she had inherited between £30,000 and £40,000 from him). He says he was reckoned in America cunning rather than able, and extremely corrupt. He had been a projector and encourager of the Stamp Act,

and had himself received a salary or poundage for distributing stamps, and it is believed that he would have been equally active in promoting the Tea Act if it had been made his interest to do so.

195.   These and many other things to the disadvantage of Franklin were told us by Hammond, but it must be considered that, as the English Minister, he most probably saw principally the Americans most attached to the interests of England, and that they would think that the abuse or depreciation of Franklin would be an agreeable topic to him. He says it is acknowledged that Franklin was much inferior in abilities to those joined with him at Paris, and particularly to Jay; that he was very vain, of which he had seen many instances. One day when at dinner with him, his French servant announced to him three Swiss gentlemen who had come all the way from Switzerland to see "*the venerable Franklin.*" The old man immediately smoothed back his grey locks and went out to them, and on his return said to Hammond, "Mr. Hammond, you have no idea how much trouble I have of this sort; people come to me in this way at almost every hour."

196.   On another occasion as Hammond was airing with him in his coach a crowd gathered hallooing, "*C'est là le grand Franklin,*" on which he immediately set himself forward in the carriage, and continued in that way, *en spectacle,* till they got home.

197.   I believe I have not before mentioned in this journal that I was present at the Cockpit, being then studying the law at Lincoln's Inn, after my return from Paris, when [Alexander] Wedderburn pronounced his celebrated philippic against Franklin, on the occasion of the petition for the removal of Governor [Thomas] Hutchinson. It was a finished and a bitter oration, and properly to be likened to some of Cicero's philippics against Anthony. Those are often thought to have cost Cicero his life, and that of Wedderburn has been considered by many as the immediate cause of the American Rebellion. During the speech he certainly stood as unmoved as a rock, and I have heard, in contradiction to the notion that he resented so unconquerably the acrimony of Wedderburn's declaration, that, on going out of the Council Chamber, he said to some of his friends that it was a most eloquent and masterly performance.

For a contrary version, see 97.

The next six anecdotes are from the autobiography John Adams wrote in 1802, ed. L. H. Butterfield, *Diary and Autobiography of JA*, 4 vols. (1961).

198.   The Taverns were so full We could with difficulty obtain Entertainment. At [New] Brunswick, but one bed could be procured for Dr. Franklin and me, in a Chamber little larger than the bed, without a Chimney and with only one small Window. The Window was open, and I, who was an invalid and afraid of the Air in the night, shut it close. Oh! says Franklin dont shut the Window. We shall be suffocated. I answered I was afraid of the Evening Air. Dr. Franklin replied, the Air within this Chamber will soon be, and indeed is now worse than that without Doors: come! open the Window and come to bed, and I will convince you: I believe you are not acquainted with my Theory of Colds. Opening the Window and leaping into Bed, I said I had read his Letters to Dr. [Samuel] Cooper in which he had advanced, that Nobody ever got cold by going into a cold Church, or any other cold Air: but the Theory was so little consistent with my experience, that I thought it a Paradox: However I had so much curiosity to hear his reasons, that I would run the risque of a cold. The Doctor then began an harrangue, upon Air and cold and Respiration and Perspiration, with which I was so much amused that I soon fell asleep, and left him and his Philosophy together: but I believe they were equally sound and insensible, within a few minutes after me, for the last Words I heard were pronounced as if he was more than half asleep.

> This was on the night of 9 September 1776, when BF, JA, and Edward Rutledge were on their way from Philadelphia to Staten Island to meet Admiral Lord Howe on terms for peace (3:418).

199.   Two or three Circumstances ... not thought worth notice in any of my private Letters, I afterwards found circulated in Europe, and oftener repeated than any other Part of this whole Transaction. Lord How[e] was profuse in his Expressions of Gratitude to the State of Massachusetts, for erecting a marble Monument in Westminster Abbey to his Elder Brother Lord How[e] who was killed in America in the last French War, saying "he esteemed that Honour to his Family, *above all Things in this World.* That such was his gratitude and affection to this Country, on that Account, that he felt for America, as for a Brother, and if America should fall, he should feel

and lament it, like the Loss of a Brother." Dr. Franklin, with an easy Air and a collected Countenance, a Bow, a Smile and all that Naivetee which sometimes appeared in his Conversation and is often observed in his Writings, replied "My Lord, We will do our Utmost Endeavours, to save your Lordship that mortification."

> 3:422. This is an expansion of Benjamin Rush's account, 79.

200.   Mr. Franklin who at the age of seventy odd, had neither lost his Love of Beauty nor his Taste for it called Mademoiselle De Passy his favourite and his flame and his Love and his Mistress, which flattered the Family and did not displease the young lady. After the Marquis had demanded Mademoiselle for a Wife and obtained her, Madam Chaumont, who was a Wit, the first time she saw Franklin cryed out "Helas! tous les Conducteurs de Monsieur Franklin, n'ont pas pu empeche le Tonnere de tomber sur Mademoiselle de Passi."

> In Adams's autobiography, dated 18 April 1778 (4:64). The French pun may be translated, "Alas! all Mr. Franklin's lightning rods could not protect Mlle de Passy from lightning": she had married the Marquis de Tonnerre.

201.   After dinner We went to the Accademy of Sciences, and heard Mr. D'Alembert as Secretary perpetual, pronounce Eulogies on several of their Members lately deceased. Voltaire and Franklin were both present, and there presently arose a general Cry that Monsieur Voltaire and Monsieur Franklin should be introduced to each other. This was done and they bowed and spoke to each other. This was no Satisfaction. There must be something more. Neither of our Philosophers seemed to divine what was wished or expected. They however took each other by the hand. . . . [sic] But this was not enough. The Clamour continued, untill the explanation came out "Il faut s'embrasser, a la francoise." The two Aged Actors upon this great Theatre of Philosophy and frivolity then embraced each other by hugging one another in their Arms and kissing each others cheeks, and then the tumult subsided. And the Cry immediately spread through the whole Kingdom and I suppose over all Europe "Qu'l etoit charmant. Oh! il etoit enchantant, de voir Solon et Sophocles embrassans." How charming it was! Oh! it was enchanting to see Solon and Sophocles embracing!

> Adams noted the event in his diary for 29 April 1778 (2:307)

and in full in his autobiography (4:80–81). For Condorcet's variant, see *169*.

202.   Franklin told Us one of his Characteristic Stories. A Spanish Writer of certain Vissions of Hell, relates that a certain evil Spirit he met with who was civil and well bred, shewed him all the Apartments in the place. Among others that of deceased Kings. The Spaniard was much amused at so illustrious a Sight, and after viewing them for sometime, said he should be glad to see the rest of them. The rest? said the Daemon. Here are all the Kings who ever reigned upon earth from the creation of it to this day, what the Devil would the Man have?

Entry dated 6 May 1778 (4:91).

203.   Franklin delighted in New Gate Anecdotes and he told us one of a Taylor who stole a horse, was detected and committed to New Gate, where he met another Felon, who had long followed the Trade of Horse Stealing. The Taylor told his Story to the other who enquired, why he had not taken such a road, and assumed such a disguise and why he had not disguised the Horse? I did not think of it. Did not think of it? Who are You? and what has been your Employment? A Taylor. . . . You never stole a Horse before I suppose in your Life? Never. . . .— What Business had you with Horse Stealing? Why did not you content yourself with your Cabbage?

Entry dated 20 May 1778 (4:105). The ellipses are in the original. For another Newgate anecdote see *51*.

204.   That Dr. Franklin, notwithstanding he did not shew it at the time, was much impressed by the business of the privy council, appeared from this circumstance:—when he attended there, he was dressed in a suit of Manchester velvet; and Silas Dean told me, that when they met at Paris, to sign the treaty between France and America, he purposely put on that suit.

Letter by Joseph Priestley, *Monthly Magazine*, 15 (1803), rpt., W. T. Franklin, *Memoirs of BF* (1818), 1:356–360. In the second edition, W. T. Franklin added a note from the former secretary of the American commissioners, Edward Bancroft, supplying an expanded version of the story about the velvet suit BF wore to the French treaty. Bancroft concludes: "I once intimated to Dr.

Franklin the suspicion which his wearing these clothes on that occasion had excited in my mind, when he smiled, without telling me whether it was well or ill founded.— I have heard him sometimes say, that he was not insensible to injuries, but that he never put himself to any trouble or inconvenience to retaliate" (2d ed. [1818], 1:357n–359n). For variants, see *111* and *128*.

205.   Dr. Franklin when a young man was in the habit of writing his name with a flourish. An old man who saw it by accident cried out, "What fool's name is this?" Ever afterwards the Doctor wrote his name in a plain and simple manner.

Letter by Benjamin Rush to his son, 22 June 1803 (L. H. Butterfield, ed., *Letters of BR*, 2 vols. [1951], 2:869).

206.   Dr. Franklin once examining a boy at the request of his father, relative to the progress he had made in his learning, found him offering *excuses* for almost every thing which he should have done. This he listened to for some time with great patience, and very much to the boy's satisfaction, who thought he had deceived him: at last he said, in his usual grave manner: "I grant you, young gentleman, you have been very *ingenious* in your apologies for not doing your duty; and as such I must report you to your father: but this I must likewise tell him as well as you,— that the boy who is *good at excuses*, is generally *good for nothing else.*"

For variant, see *220*.

207.   When people who had got together a little money in trade, used to be capriciously wishing to live in the country (without having a single quality or habit to fit them for agriculture, its pursuit, or enjoyments), he would drily ask, "What do you think of the country for?" The answer usually was, "Oh! because I am *tired* of the town."— "And for this reason," replied he, "you want to *re-tire* in the country."

208.   When he heard people say "they were tired of a thing," merely through a want of proper perseverance, he used to reply, "Well, do as married people do; *tire* and *begin again.*"

209.   When any one was for proving the fortune and respectability of another by the number of servants, carriages, etc. the Doctor used to reply, "Well, well; this may be your opinion, and the opinion

of many people: but I have not yet learnt that *extravagance* is the criterion of *fortune* or *independence.*"

London jestbook, *Memoirs of Sam Foote*, 3 vols. (1805), 3:64–71.

210.   Dr. Franklin received me without any ceremony, but with the kindness of a parent; and in this way he conducted himself towards all the Americans, whom he was in the habit of calling his children. I found in company with him, the Marquis de la Fayette, and several other gentlemen: and as soon as they were gone (which was in about half an hour after my arrival) the Doctor asked me to follow him into his study . . . and gave me good advice, relative to the conduct which I ought to observe while I resided at Paris, and in the same familiar style as though he had been my father, and for which I shall always revere him as long as I live.

> *Memoirs of the Life of Captain Nathaniel Fanning* (1806), a midshipman under John Paul Jones, rpt., *Magazine of History*, extra no. 21 (1913), p. 214. The last sentence was transformed by Herman Melville into chaps. 7–11 of *Israel Potter*, serialized in *Putnam's Monthly Magazine* for August-September 1854 (4:142–146, 277–285).

211.   Some years since, as doctor Franklin was travelling through New-England, he, on a winter's evening, alighted at a tavern, and ordered his horse to be stabled. To the doctor's mortification, he found there was but one room in the house accommodated with a fire, and that this was so engrossed by indolent countrymen that he could not approach it. To obtain the benefit of the fire, was an object of importance to a traveller shivering with the cold, and this was effected by the following device. "Landlord (said the doctor) have you *oysters?*" "Yes, Sir." "Give my *horse* an half bushel of them." Sir! *oysters! your horse* an half bushel of *oysters?*" "Yes, sir, give him the oysters." The guest was obeyed; and as this discourse did not escape the attention of the countrymen, *curiosity* prompted them to repair to the stable to see in *what manner* the horse would eat oysters. The doctor rejoiced in their absence, and seated himself by the fire. But a few minutes, however, passed before the men returned, when the host thus exclaimed: *"Sir, your horse won't eat the oysters!"* "Will he not? (said the doctor) O then bring them here and roast them; they will answer for *my supper.*" The *loungers* had sagacity sufficient to discern the wit and

intention of the traveller, and, not being entirely devoid of shame, they soon, by degrees, sneaked off, and left the philosopher in a very comfortable situation.

> New York jestbook, *American Magazine of Wit* (1808), p. 58. This is an old favorite of the jestbooks: in the London *Treasury of Wit* (1786) the hero is merely "a merry fellow" (2:213); in the Worcester, Mass., *Funny Stories* (1795), he is "a merry conceited Parson riding from London to Colchester" (pp. 97–98), but he was a "merry Fellow" also as early as 1637–1655 (*Merry Passages and Jeasts*, p. 77).

212.   At the conclusion of the late war, Dr. Franklin, the English Ambassador, and the French Minister Vergennes, dining together, at Versailles, a toast from each was called for, and agreed to. The British Minister began with "George the third, who, like the *sun* in its meridian, spreads a lustre throughout, and enlightens the world." The French Minister followed with, "the illustrious Louis the 16th, who, like the *moon*, sheds its mild and benignant rays on, and influences the globe." Our American Franklin then gives, "George Washington commander of the American armies; who, (like Joshua of old) commanded the *sun* and *moon to stand still*, and they obeyed him."

> *American Magazine of Wit* (1808), p. 68, another jestbook favorite, with the hero most frequently the Earl of Stair, Britain's ambassador to Holland (e.g., *Tell Tale* [1756], 2:257–258), or the Earl of Chesterfield (*New Theatre of Fun* [1778], p. 36). For a later variant, see *241*.

213.   Mr. Smith told [Thomas Jefferson] the ladies *would* follow him. "That is right," said he, "since I am too old to follow them. I remember in France when his friends were taking leave of Dr. Franklin, the ladies smothered him with embraces and on his introducing me to them as his successor, I told him I wished he would transfer these privileges to me, but he answered, 'You are too young a man.'"

> Letter by Margaret Bayard Smith to her sister-in-law, March 1809, ed. Gaillard Hunt, *First Forty Years of Washington Society* (1906), p. 59.

214.   Dr. Franklin told me, that before his return to America from England, in 1775, he was in company, I believe at Lord Spencer's

[Le Despencer], with a number of English noblemen, when the conversation turned upon fables, those of Aesop, LaFontaine, Gay, Moore, etc. etc. Some one of the company observed that he thought the subject was exhausted. He did not believe that any man could now find an animal, beast, bird, or fish, that he could work into a new fable with any success; and the whole company appeared to applaud the idea, except Franklin, who was silent. The gentleman insisted on his opinion. He said, with submission to their lordships, he believed the subject was inexhaustible, and that many new and instructive fables might be made out of such materials. Can you think of any one at present? If your lordship will furnish me a pen, ink, and paper, I believe I can furnish your lordship with one in a few minutes. The paper was brought, and he sat down and wrote.—

"Once upon a time, an eagle scaling around a farmer's barn, and espying a hare, darted down upon him like a sunbeam, seized him in his claws, and remounted with him in the air. He soon found that he had a creature of more courage and strength than a hare, for which, notwithstanding the keenness of his eyesight, he had mistaken a cat. The snarling and scrambling of the prey was very inconvenient, and, what was worse, she had disengaged herself from his talons, grasped his body with her four limbs, so as to stop his breath, and seized fast hold of his throat with her teeth. Pray, said the eagle, let go your hold, and I will release you. Very fine, said the cat, I have no fancy to fall from this height and be crushed to death. You have taken me up, and you shall stoop and let me down. The eagle thought it necessary to stoop accordingly."

The moral was so applicable to England and America, that the fable was allowed to be original, and highly applauded.

John Adams in the *Boston Patriot*, June 1809, ed., C. F. Adams, *Words of JA*, 10 vols. (1856), 9:268–269. The draft of this version is in JA's diary, dated 3 November 1782, ed., L. H. Butterfield, *Diary and Autobiography of JA*, 4 vols. (1961), 3:45: "The present Conduct of England and America resembles that of the Eagle and Cat. An Eagle scaling over a Farmer's Yard espied a Creature, that he thought an Hair. He pounced upon him and took him up. In the Air the Cat seized him by the Neck with her Teeth and round the Body with her fore and hind Claws. The Eagle finding Herself scratched and pressed, bids the Cat let go and fall down.— No says the Cat: I won't let go and fall, you shall stoop and set me down." For BF's own version, see *20*.

215.   Dr. Franklin probably had his share of jealousy and dislike towards [the Cincinnati]; but did not choose to give explicit judgment against a proceeding, which was generally popular and countenanced by a great part of the best citizens. The Marquis de la Fayette, with whom it was a favourite project, in company with the doctor, said, "Pray sir, what is your opinion of the establishment of the Cincinnati?" "Why truly, Marquis," said the doctor slily, "I have no opinion of it at all."

> Federalist magazine, the *Monthly Anthology and Boston Review*, 7 (September 1809): 174.

216.   Soon after the establishment of his paper, a person brought him a piece, which he requested him to publish in the Pennsylvania Gazette. Franklin desired that the piece might be left for his consideration until next day, when he would give an answer. The person returned at the time appointed, and received from Franklin this communication, "I have perused your piece, and find it to be scurrilous and defamatory,— to determine whether I should publish it or not, I went home in the evening, purchased a twopenny loaf at the baker's, and, with water from the pump made my supper;— I then wrapped myself up in my great coat, and laid down on the floor and slept till morning, when on another loaf and a mug of water, I made my breakfast. From this regimen I feel no inconvenience whatever. Finding I can live in this manner, I have formed a determination never to prostitute my press to the purposes of corruption, and abuse of this kind, for the sake of gaining a more comfortable subsistence."

> Isaiah Thomas, *History of Printing in America*, 2 vols. (1810), 2:43.

217.   Doctor Franklin used to say, "The maxim of not speaking evil of the dead should be reversed. We should speak evil *only* of the dead, for in so doing we can do them no harm. We hurt the living only by exposing their vices."

> Letter by Benjamin Rush to James Cheetham, 6 January 1810, ed. L. H. Butterfield, *Letters of BR*, 2 vols. (1951), 2:1034.

218.   I returned from France in December, 1789, and in March following I went on to New York to take the post assigned me in the new government. On my way through Philadelphia I called on Dr.

Franklin, who was then confined to his bed. As the revolution had then begun, indeed was supposed to be closed by the completion of a constitution, and he was anxious to know the part all his acquaintances had taken, he plied me with questions for an hour or two with a vivacity and earnestness which astonished me. When I had satisfied his inquiries, I observed to him that I had heard, and with great pleasure, that he had begun the history of his own life, and had brought it down to the revolution (for so I had heard while in Europe). "Not exactly so," said he, "but I will let you see the manner in which I do these things." He then desired one of his small grandchildren who happened to be in the room, to bring him such a paper from the table. It was brought, and he put it into my hands and said, "There, put that into your pocket and you will see the manner of my writing." I thanked him and said, "I shall read it with great pleasure, and return it to him safely." "No," said he, "keep it." I took it with me to New York. It was, as well as I recollect, about a quire of paper, in which he had given, with great minuteness, all the details of his negotiations (informal) in England, to prevent their pushing us to extremities.

> Letter from Thomas Jefferson to William Duane, 16 September 1810, ed. A. A. Lipscomb, *Writings of TJ*, 20 vols. (1903-1905), 12:414-415; revised version by TJ is in his autobiography, ed. P. L. Ford, *Writings of TJ*, 10 vols. (1892-1899), 1:150-151.

219.   I remember, [said Dr. Franklin,] that in America I once drew up a paper for adoption at a public meeting, and after it was read, a carpenter took it into his hands, and dividing the sheet into two, said of one leaf, *This I think is enough, and will answer.*—

> Unpublished letter by Benjamin Vaughan, 6 May 1811 in the American Philosophical Society Library, BV, 46p.

220.   A young man having broken an appointment with Dr. Franklin, came to him the following day, and made a very handsome apology for his absence: He was proceeding when the doctor stopped him with, "My good boy, say no more, you have said too much already; for the man who is so *good* at making an excuse, is seldom *good at any thing else.*"

> Variant of 206.

221.   The late Dr. Franklin used to observe, that of all the amusements which the ingenuity of man had ever devised for the purpose of *recreation*, none required the exercise of most patient attention so much as *angling*: a remark which he frequently illustrated by the following story:

About six o'clock on a fine morning in the summer (said the doctor), I set out from Philadelphia on a visit to a friend at the distance of fifteen miles, and passing a brook where a gentleman was angling, I inquired if he had caught any thing? "No, sir (said he), I have not been here long; only two hours." I wished him a good morning, and pursued my journey. On my return in the evening, I found him fixed to the identical spot where I had left him, and again enquired if he had any sport? "Very good, sir," says he. "Caught a great many fish?" "None at all." "Had a great many bites though, I suppose?" "Not one, but I had a most glorious nibble!!!"

Chaplet of Comus, Boston jestbook (1811), pp. 29–30, 246.

222.   I recollect he once told me that a large sum of money passed through his hands for the purchase of stores for the British army during the last French war in America. When he settled his accounts with the quartermaster of the army, he said to him, "I wait now for my commissions." "Commissions," said the Quartermaster, "Why, have you not paid yourself?" "No, sir, you see from the statement of my accounts I have not," said the Doctor. "I am sorry for it," said the Quartermaster; "I have no power to allow you anything. You ought to have taken care of *yourself*."

Letter by Benjamin Rush to John Adams, 19 August 1811, ed. L. H. Butterfield, *Letters of BR*, 2 vols. (1951), 2:1093–1094. This echoes a passage in BF's *Autobiography* (NCE pp. 417–418): "On my observing that . . . I charg'd no Commissions for my Service: O, Sir, says [Lord Loudon], you must not think of persuading us that you are no Gainer. We understand better those Affairs, and know that every one concern'd in supplying the Army finds means in the doing it to fill his own Pockets."

223.   In 1775 Franklin made a morning Visit, at Mrs. Yards to Sam Adams and John. He was unusually loquacious. "Man, a rational Creature!" said Franklin. "Come, Let Us suppose a rational Man. Strip him of all his Appetites, especially of his hunger and thirst. He

is in his Chamber, engaged in making Experiments, or in pursuing some Problem. He is highly entertained. At this moment a Servant Knocks, "Sir dinner is on Table." "Dinner! Pox! Pough! But what have you for dinner?" "Ham and Chickens." "Ham! And must I break the chain of my thoughts, to go down and knaw a morsel of a damn'd Hogs Arse? Put aside your Ham. I will dine tomorrow."

> Letter by John Adams to Thomas Jefferson, 15 November 1813, ed. L. J. Cappon, *Adams-Jefferson Letters*, 2 vols. (1959), 2:399.

 The next three anecdotes are from the first version of BF's biography by Mason L. ("Parson") Weems. His *Life of BF, Written Chiefly by Himself* (1815), largely a reprinting of the *Autobiography* as it had appeared in 1793, contained a few interpolations of Weems's anecdotes. Completely rewritten in 1818 as the *Life of BF, with Many Choice Anecdotes*, the interpolations overwhelmed the original narrative. Examples from the later edition are included in their proper chronological position in *237-242*.

224.   "How many beatitudes are there, Ben?" said his father to Franklin, when but a *boy*, and just from school. *Nine, sir;* replied Ben with his usual promptness: *but I wish, father, there had been one more.* "And pray, Ben, what would you have that to be?" *Why, sir, blessed are they that are out of debt, and have money to lend to their poor friends.*

Page 96.

225.   His experiments in electricity, with which he used daily to entertain the crowding citizens, were well calculated to keep alive their astonishment at his powers, which to many good people appeared but little short of conjuration. And here let me mention:
I.   The Magic Pistol.   In the presence of a large party at his house, he took up a pistol, which he had beforehand charged with inflammable air, well stopped with a cork, and presented it to Miss Leaton, a celebrated belle in those days. She took it from the Doctor, but could not help turning pale, as though some conjuration was abrewing. *"Don't be afraid, madam,"* said he, *"for I give you my word that there is not a grain of powder in it; and now turn it against any gentleman in the room that you are angry with."* With a sudden blush,

she turned it towards a gentleman whom she soon after married. In the same instant the doctor drew a charged rod near the mouth of the pistol, the electric spark rushed in, and set fire to the inflammable air; off went the pistol; out flew the cork, and striking her lover a smart shock in the face, fell down on the floor, to the exceeding terror at first, but afterwards, to the equal diversion of the young lady and the whole company.

II.   The Dancing Dogs. At another time, in a large party at his house, all eager, as usual, to see some of his Electrical Curiosities, he took from the drawer a number of little dogs made of the pith of elder with straw for feet and tails, and set them on the table. All eyes were fixed on him. *"Well, Miss Eliza,"* said he, addressing the elegant Miss E. Sitgreaves, *"can you set these little dogs a-dancing?"* No, indeed, can't I, replied she. *"Well,"* replied he, *"if I had such a pair of eyes as you have, I think I could do it."* She blushed. *"However, let us see,"* continued he, *"if we can't do something."* He then took a large tumbler from the table, which he had previously charged with the electric fluid, and very gravely muttering a sentence or two of strange outlandish words, like one *pow-wowing*, he clapped the tumbler over the dogs; whereupon they instantly fell to skipping and jumping up the sides of the tumbler, as if they were half mad to get out of it. . . .

Sometimes he would place a young lady, generally the handsomest of the company, on his electrical stool; then by slily touching her dress with his magic wand, he would so fill her lovely frame with the electric fluid, that, on the approach of any young gentleman to kiss her, a spark from her ruby lips would suddenly drive him frightened and staggering back. This was called the Magic Kiss.

Pages 107–108, 110.

226.   The elegant [John] Dickinson, Esq. informed me that he was at doctor Franklin's, one evening, with a very large party, when a dreadful black cloud began to rise, with distant thunder and lightning. The ladies, panic struck as usual, were all in a prodigious bustle for their bonnets, to get home. The doctor intreated them not to be frightened; for that they were in the safest house in Philadelphia; and indeed, jokingly, offered to underwrite their lives at the low premium of a groat a head.

Pages 114–115.

227.   One evening, after a burst of laughter at some scene, [Miss Gunn] drawn by his folly-painting humour, asked him if he never wrote verses.

He replied in the negative.

"O, I am certain you can, doctor Franklin; for you just now made a beautiful couplet."

"Well then, madam, it must have been by *accident*; for I have never tried to make even a jingle, since I was a poor *printer's boy."*

"Ah," said she laughing, *"did not I say you had made verses? And now I insist, doctor Franklin, that you make me a verse off hand."* . . .

"Well, madam, since every body is complimenting your beauty, I will try my hand, and in this way:

> Cupid now, to insure his fun,
> Quits his bow, and takes to Gun."

Pages 135–136. Beauties named "Gunn" and "Gunning" were the delights of jestbook poets; e.g.,

Sly Cupid, perceiving our modern beaux' hearts
Were proof to the sharpest and best of his darts,
His power to maintain, the young urchin, grown cunning,
Has laid down his bow, and now conquers by Gunning.

(H. P. Dodd, *The Epigrammatists* [1889], p. 571). I very much doubt that BF made the verse.

228.   Dr. Franklin had occasion, in company with an English-man to mention Lord Cholmondely, which he pronounced as spelled. The Englishman burst into a boisterous laugh, and informed the Doctor that it should be pronounced *Shumley.—* Without seeming to notice the Englishman's impoliteness, the Doctor calmly inquired if there were not families in London who spelled their name, C, u, n, n, i, n, g, h, a, m? "Yes," replied the Englishman, "several." "Pray, sir, how do you pronounce their name?" "Why Cunningham, to be sure, *as it is spelled."* "Well," observed the Doctor, it is very fortunate for me, that you did not pronounce it so in my presence, when I was a little ignorant soap-boiler's apprentice: for I should probably have then been silly enough to have laughed in your face; as we in Boston always pronounced it *Kinninkum.*

American Yeoman, 13 May 1817, rpt., M. B. Péladeau, *Prose of Royall Tyler* (1972), p. 330, where it is attributed to Tyler, who was responsible also for *179* and *180*. Another of his may be an often reprinted short story about BF trying a "scientific experiment" to see if his own mother would recognize him after a long absence—which James Parton called an "incredible" tale (*Life of BF*, 2 vols. [1865], 1:618–621). Among a number of "Moral Tales" that Tyler listed in 1800, one was entitled, "Dr. Franklin and His Mother: a Philosophical Experiment" (Péladeau, p. 458).

229.   When I was in London studying painting with Mr. [Benjamin] West . . . I wanted to be introduced to Doctor Franklin, and not knowing who I could ask the favour of an introduction to the Doctor I determined one day to call on him—and enquiring where he lodged I went alone to the House, being shewn into the Room where he was sitting with a young Lady on his knee, and in the dress of the Picture now in the Room of the Philosophical society in Philadelphia. . . . The Doctor was very friendly to me, shewed me his experiments which he was then making, and desired me to call on him at any of my leisure moments and he would be always glad to see me.

> Diary of painter Charles Willson Peale, referring to 1767, rpt., C. C. Sellers, *BF in Portraiture* (1962), p. 81, with a pencil sketch supposed to show the scene of BF with the young lady on his knee.

230.   I passed one day with Dr. Franklin at Spithead, with Sir [Joseph] Banks and the late Dr. [Daniel] Solander (one of the most pleasant men I ever met with), when they went to smooth the water with oil. Lord Loughborough [Alexander Wedderburn] was of the party. I remember there was but little conversation, except from Solander, and a laughable scene between an officer on board the ship and Dr. Franklin, on the properties of thunder and lightning.— The officer continually contradicted the Doctor with saying, "Sir, you are quite wrong in your opinion; Dr. Franklin says so and so; the Doctor and you are quite contrary in your ideas. I never will allow, sir, that Dr. F. is wrong. No, Sir; I am sure he is right, and you are wrong, begging your pardon." The Doctor never altered a feature at the conversation. All the company enjoyed a laugh except the disputants.

> *Memoirs of . . . John Coakley Lettsom*, ed. T. J. Pettigrew, 3 vols. (1817), 1:175–176, widely reprinted; for example (Boston) *Athe-*

neum, 3 (1818): 327. BF's own report of the trip in 1773 does mention Banks and Solander, but certainly not Wedderburn, his antagonist in 1774, nor the sailor (P 20:471–474).

231.   This philosopher dined one day in Paris with several academicians at the home of a distinguished lady. The mistress showed him to her son, who was about 8 or 9, high-spirited and already versed in some features of Roman history. "My dear," said the mother, "pay attention to monsieur because he is a great man.—" "Mama, what is a great man?" "My son, he is a man who does great things." "What does 'great things' mean?" "You will see for yourself when we are at table." The child meditated a moment or two, looking fixedly at Franklin. "My dear mama," he cried with joy, "I know who that man is! Isn't he Brutus?"

232.   When he was in England, Doctor Franklin was walking in the London streets with his spectacles on his nose. One of his friends asked why he did not take them off. "O," said the philosopher, "they often help me to see." A moment later, they met a porter and Franklin bumped against him. The porter, taking three steps back, cursed: "The devil take your spectacles!" And Franklin said to his friend: "You see? I told you my spectacles helped me. Without them, he would have damned my eyes."

> Parisian jestbook, *Frankliniana* (no date, but probably about 1818), pp. 51–52, 65–66. The story of the spectacles appeared in the English *Encyclopedia of Wit* (1805), p. 328.

 The next four anecdotes are among the seven "Anecdotes Relative to Dr. Franklin," ed. William Temple Franklin, *Memoirs of BF* (1818), 1:447–449.

233.   When Franklin came to England previous to the breaking out of the American war, he went to Mr. [Richard] Hett's Printing Office in Wild Court, Wild Street, Lincoln's Inn Fields, and entering the Press-room, he went up to a particular press, and thus addressed the two men who were working. "Come, my friends, we will drink together; it is now 40 years since I worked like you at this press as a journeyman printer"— on this he sent for a gallon of porter, and they drank "success to printing."

> Richard Hett was successor to BF's old master, John Watts, who died in 1763.

234.   In one of the assemblies in America, wherein there was a majority of Presbyterians, a law was proposed to forbid the praying for the King by the Episcopalians; who, however, could not conveniently omit that prayer, it being prescribed in their Liturgy. Dr. Franklin, one of the members, seeing that such a law would occasion more disturbance than it was worth, said, that he thought it quite *unnecessary*; for, added he, "those people have, to my certain knowledge, been praying constantly these twenty years past, that '*God would give to the King and his counsel wisdom,*' and we all know that not the least notice has ever been taken of that prayer; so that it is plain they have no interest in the court of Heaven." The house smiled, and the motion was dropt.

> This could have happened during the Pennsylvania Constitutional Convention, 15 July–28 September 1776, when BF served as its president.

235.   In Philadelphia, where there are no *Noblesse*, but the inhabitants are all either merchants or mechanics, the merchants, many years since, set up an assembly for dancing, and desiring to make a distinction, and to assume a rank above the mechanics, they at first proposed this among the rules for regulating the assembly, "that *no mechanic or mechanic's wife or daughter should be admitted, on any terms.*" These rules being shown by a manager to Dr. Franklin for his opinion, he remarked, that one of them excluded God Almighty. *How so?* said the manager. "Because," replied the Doctor, "*he is notoriously the greatest mechanic in the universe*; having, as the Scripture testifies, made all things, and that by *weight* and *measure.*" The intended *new gentlemen* became ashamed of their rule, and struck it out.

> BF's own daughter was excluded from Presidential levees after his death, and his grandson was denied admittance to the Philadelphia assembly because he was a printer, according to William Duane's "postliminary preface," *Memoirs of BF*, 2 vols. (1834–1840), 1:xxxi.

236.   Dr. Franklin was so immoderately fond of chess, that one evening at Passy, he sat at that amusement from six in the afternoon till sun-rise. On the point of losing one of his games, his *king* being attacked, by what is called a check, but an opportunity offering at the

same time of giving a fatal blow to his adversary, provided he might neglect the defence of his king, he chose to do so, though contrary to the rules, and made his move. "Sir," said the French gentleman, his antagonist, "you cannot do that, and leave your king *in check.*" "I see he is in check," said the Doctor, "but I shall not defend him. If he was a good king like yours, he would deserve the protection of his subjects; but he is a tyrant and has cost them already more than he is worth:— Take him, if you please; I can do without him, and will fight out the rest of the battle, *en Républicain*— as a Commonwealth's man."

 The next six anecdotes are from Mason L. Weems, *Life of BF with Many Choice Anecdotes* (1818); page references are to the Philadelphia reprint of 1835.

237.   [BF's] good old uncle Benjamin used to divert his friends with another story, which happened in the family of his own aunt, who kept an inn at Eaton, Northamptonshire.

A most violent priest, of the name of Asquith, who thought, like Saul, that he should be doing *"God service"* by killing the heretics, had obtained letters patent from queen Mary against those people in the county of Warwick. On his way he called to dine at Eaton, where he was quickly waited on by the mayor, a strong catholic, to ask how the *good work went on.* Asquith, leaping to his saddle-bags, drew forth a little box, that contained his commission, which he flourished before the mayor, exclaiming with high glee, *"Aye! there's that that will scorch the rogues!"* Old Mrs. Franklin, under the rose a sturdy protestant, overhearing this, was exceedingly troubled; and watching her opportunity when the priest had stepped out with the mayor, slipped the commission out of the box, and put in its place a pack of cards, wrapped in the same paper. The priest returning in haste, and suspecting no trick, huddled up his box, and posted off for Coventry. A grand council of the saints was speedily convoked to meet him. He arose, and having with great vehemence delivered a set speech against the heretics, threw his commission on the table for the secretary to read aloud. With the eyes of the whole council on him, the eager secretary opened the package, when in place of the flaming commission, behold a pack of cards with the knave of clubs turned uppermost!

Pages 8–9. All Parson Weems did was substitute the fictitious "Aunt Franklin" for a nameless woman of Chester in a well-known story about Henry Cole, one of Queen Mary's commissioners, authenticated by Robert Ware, *Historical Collections of the Church in Ireland* (1681), p. 17. The nameless woman lived on in the jestbooks: as late as 1871 in the *London Jester*, pp. 146–147.

238.   [BF] would often repeat in the company of young people, the following anecdote which he had picked up some where or other in his extensive reading. "A wealthy citizen of Athens, who had nearly ruined his constitution by gluttony and sloth, was advised by Hippocrates to visit a certain medicinal spring in Sparta; not that Hippocrates believed that spring to be better than some nearer home; but *exercise* was the object— "*Visit the springs of Sparta*," said the great physician. As the young debauchee, pale and bloated, travelled among the simple and hardy Spartans, he called one day at the house of a countryman on the road to get something to eat. A young woman was just serving up dinner— a nice barn-door fowl boiled with a piece of fat bacon. "You have got rather a plain dinner there madam," growled the Athenian. "Yes, sir," replied the young woman blushing, "*but my husband will be here directly, and he always brings the sauce with him.*" Presently the young husband stepped in, and after welcoming his guest, invited him to dinner. "I can't dream of dining, sir, *without sauce*," said the Athenian, "and your wife promised you would bring it." "*O, sir, my wife is a wit*," cried the Spartan; "*she only meant the good appetite which I always bring with me from the barn, where I have been threshing.*"

Page 15.

239.   At a learned table in Paris, where Dr. Franklin happened to dine, it was asked by the abbé Raynal, *What description of men most deserves pity?*"

Some mentioned one character, and some another. When it came to Franklin's turn, he replied, *A lonesome man in a rainy day, who does not know how to read.*

Pages 17–18.

240.   Doctor Franklin observing one day a hearty young fellow, whom he knew to be an extraordinary blacksmith, sitting on the wharf, bobbing for little mud-cats and eels, he called to him, "Ah

Tom, what a pity 'tis you don't fish with a *silver* hook." The young man replied, "he was not able to fish with a silver hook." Some days after this, the doctor passing that way, saw Tom out at the end of the wharf again, with his long pole bending over the flood. "What, Tom," cried the doctor, "have you not got the silver hook yet?"

"God bless you, doctor," cried the blacksmith, "I'm hardly able to fish with an iron hook."

"Poh! poh!" replied the doctor, "go home to your anvil; and you'll make silver enough in one day to buy more and better fish than you would catch here in a month."

Page 154.

241.   When Dr. Franklin was received at the French court as American minister, he felt some scruples of conscience in complying with their *fashions as to dress*. "He hoped," he said to the minister, "that as he was himself a very plain man, and represented a plain republican people, the king would indulge his desire to appear at court in his usual dress. Independent of this, the season of the year, he said, rendered the change from warm yarn stockings to fine silk, somewhat dangerous."

The French minister made him a bow, but said, that *The Fashion* was too sacred a thing for him to meddle with, but he would do himself the honour to mention it to his *Majesty*.

The king smiled, and returned word that Dr. Franklin was welcome to appear at court in *any dress he pleased*. In spite of that delicate respect for strangers, for which the French are so remarkable, the courtiers could not help staring, at first, at Dr. Franklin's quaker-like dress, and especially his *"Blue Yarn Stockings."* But it soon appeared as though he had been introduced upon this splendid theatre only to demonstrate that, great genius, like true beauty, "needs not the foreign aid of ornament." The court were so dazzled with the brilliancy of his mind that they never looked at his stockings.

Pages 212–213. The quotation in the next-to-last sentence is from James Thomson's *Seasons*, "Autumn," 1:205 (*Poetical Works*, ed. J. L. Robertson [1908], p. 140), which speaks about "loveliness" rather than "true beauty."

242.   The following I obtained from the Rev. Dr. Helmuth, of the German church, Philadelphia. Hearing that this learned and pious

divine possessed a valuable anecdote of doctor Franklin, I immediately waited on him. "Yes, sir," said he, "I have indeed a valuable anecdote of doctor Franklin, which I would tell you with great pleasure; but as I do not speak English very well, I wish you would call on David Ritter, at the sign of the *Golden Lamb,* in Front street; he will tell it to you better. I hastened to Mr Ritter, and told him my errand. He seemed mightily pleased at it, and said, "Yes, I will tell you all I know of it. You must understand then, sir, first of all, that I always had a prodigious opinion of doctor Franklin, as the *usefulest* man we ever had among us, by a long way; and so hearing that he was sick, I thought I would go and see him. As I rapped at the door, who should come and open it but old Sarah Humphries. I was right glad to see her, for I had known her a long time. She was of the people called *Friends;* and a mighty good sort of body she was too. The great people set a heap of store by her, for she was famous throughout the town for nursing and tending on the sick. . . . Soon as she saw me, she said, 'Well David, how dost?'

" 'O, much after the old sort, Sarah,' said I; 'but that's neither here nor there; I am come to see doctor Franklin.'

" 'Well then,' said she, 'thou art too late, for he is *just dead!*'

" 'Alack a day,' said I, 'then a great man is gone.' . . .

"She took me into his room. As we entered, she pointed to him, where he lay on his bed, and said, '*there,* did thee ever see any thing look so natural?'

"And he did look natural indeed. His eyes were closed—but that you saw he did not breathe, you would have thought he was in a sweet sleep, he looked so calm and happy. Observing that his face was fixed right towards the chimney, I cast my eyes that way, and behold! just above the mantlepiece was a noble picture! O it was a *noble picture,* sure enough! It was the picture of our Saviour on the cross.

"I could not help calling out, 'Bless us all, Sarah!' said I, 'what's all this?'

" 'What dost mean, David,' said she, quite crusty.

" 'Why, how came this picture here, Sarah?' said I, 'you know that many people think he was not after this sort.'

" 'Yes,' said she, 'I know that too. But thee knows that many who makes a great fuss about religion have very little, while some who say but little about it have a good deal.'

" 'That's sometimes the case, I fear, Sarah;' said I.

" 'Well, and that was the case,' said she, 'with Benjamin Franklin. . . . Many weeks ago, as he lay, he beckoned me to him, and told me of this picture up stairs, and begged I would bring it to him. I brought it to him. His face brightened up as he looked at it; and he said, *Aye, Sarah,* said he, *there's a picture worth looking at! that's the picture of him who came into the world to teach men to love one another!* Then after looking wistfully at it for some time, he said, *Sarah,* said he, *set this picture up over the mantlepiece, right before me as I lie; for I like to look at it,* and when I had fixed it up, he looked at it, and looked at it very much; and indeed, as thee see, he died with his eyes fixed on it."

Pages 236–237. Like the bulk of Weems's, no doubt fiction.

243.   Franklin had often declared, in the societies of Paris, that Philadelphia would not be taken by Howe. When this event was announced in the French metropolis as certain, one of the multitude of fashionable women, who, from admiration of the representative had conceived a violent attachment for the American cause, repaired in all haste to Passy, and drawing the curtains of his bed at an early hour in the morning, exclaimed, "Why, Dr. Franklin! did you not tell us that Howe would not take Philadelphia? It is positively so." "No, Madam," answered the negotiator, with an air of complacency, "there is a mistake, *it is Philadelphia that has taken Howe.*"

Delaplaine's Repository for December 1818, 2:114–115. Variant of *83* and *127.*

 The next seven anecdotes by Thomas Jefferson were composed in response to a request from Robert Walsh who was writing the sketch of BF for *Delaplaine's Repository*, with additional work in view (*Writings of TJ,* ed. A. A. Lipscomb, 20 vols. [1903], 15:176): "I state a few anecdotes of Dr. Franklin, with my own knowledge, too much in detail for the scale of Delaplaine's work, but which may find a *cadre* in some of the more particular views you contemplate." In 1815, he had turned down a similar request from Parson Weems: "I recollect nothing within my own knowledge but what the public records and gazettes will furnish with much more exactitude than could be stated from a decaying memory" (*Correspondence of TJ*, ed. W. C. Ford [1916], p. 226). The text here is from P. L. Ford, ed., *Writings of TJ*, 10 vols. (1899), 118n–121n, dated 4 December 1818.

244.   Our revolutionary process, as is well known, commenced by petitions, memorials, remonstrances, etc. from the old Congress. These were followed by a non-importation agreement, as a pacific instrument of coercion. While that was before us, and sundry exceptions, as of arms, ammunition, etc. were moved from different quarters of the house, I was sitting by Dr. Franklin and observed to him that I thought we should except books: that we ought not to exclude science, even coming from an enemy. He thought so too, and I proposed the exception, which was agreed to. Soon after it occurred that medicine should be excepted, and I suggested that also to the Doctor. "As to that," said he, "I will tell you a story. When I was in London, in such a year, there was a weekly club of Physicians, of which Sir John Pringle was president, and I was invited by my friend Dr. Fothergill to attend when convenient. Their rule was to propose a thesis one week, and discuss it the next. I happened there when the question to be considered was whether Physicians had, on the whole, done most good or harm? The young members, particularly, having discussed it very learnedly and eloquently till the subject was exhausted, one of them observed to Sir John Pringle, that, altho' it was not usual for the President to take part in a debate, yet they were desirous to know his opinion on the question. He said, they must first tell him whether, under the appellation of Physicians, they meant to include *old women*; if they did, he thought they had done more good than harm, otherwise more harm than good."

For variant, see 255.

245.   The confederation of the States, while on the carpet before the old Congress, was strenuously opposed by the smaller states, under apprehensions that they would be swallowed up by the larger ones. We were long engaged in the discussion; it produced great heats, much ill humor, and intemperate declarations from some members. Dr. Franklin at length brought the debate to a close with one of his little apologues. He observed that "at the time of the Union of England and Scotland, the Duke of Argyle was most violently opposed

to that measure, and among other things predicted that, as the whale had swallowed Jonas, so Scotland would be swallowed by England. "However," said the Doctor, "when Lord Bute came into the government, he soon brought into it's administration so many of his countrymen that it was found in event that Jonas swallowed the whale." This little story produced a general laugh, restored good humor, and the Article of difficulty was passed.

Variant of 77.

246.   When Dr. Franklin went to France on his revolutionary mission, his eminence as a philosopher, his venerable appearance, and the cause on which he was sent, rendered him extremely popular. For all ranks and conditions of men there, entered warmly into the American interest. He was therefore feasted and invited to all the court parties. At these he sometimes met the old Duchess of Bourbon, who being a chess player of about his force, they very generally played together. Happening once to put her king into prise, the Doctor took it. "Ah," says she, "we do not take kings so." "We do in America," said the Doctor.

247.   At one of these parties, the emperor Joseph II then at Paris, incognito under the title of Count Falkenstein, was overlooking the game, in silence, while the company was engaged in animated conversation on the American question. "How happens it M. le Comte," said the Duchess, "that while we all feel so much interest in the cause of the Americans, you say nothing for them?" "I am a king by trade," said he.

248.   When the Declaration of Independence was under the consideration of Congress, there were two or three unlucky expressions in it which gave offence to some members. The words "Scotch and other foreign auxiliaries" excited the ire of a gentleman or two of that country. Severe strictures on the conduct of the British king, in negativing our repeated repeals of the law which permitted the importation of slaves, were disapproved by some Southern gentlemen whose reflections were not yet matured to the full abhorrence of that traffic. Altho' the offensive expressions were immediately yielded, these gentlemen continued their depredations on other parts of the instrument. I was sitting by Dr. Franklin who perceived that I was not insensible to these mutilations. "I have made it a rule," said he, "whenever in

my power, to avoid becoming the draughtsman of papers to be re-
viewed by a public body. I took my lesson from an incident which
I will relate to you. When I was a journeyman printer, one of my
companions, an apprentice Hatter, having served out his time, was
about to open shop for himself, his first concern was to have a handsome signboard, with a proper inscription. He composed it in these
words 'John Thompson, *Hatter, makes and sells hats for ready money,*'
with a figure of a hat subjoined. But he thought he would submit it
to his friends for their amendments. The first he shewed it to thought
the word 'Hatter' tautologous, because followed by the words 'makes
hats' which shew he was a Hatter. It was struck out. The next
observed that the word 'makes' might as well be omitted, because
his customers would not care who made the hats. If good and to their
mind, they would buy by whomsoever made. He struck it out. A third
said he thought the words *'for ready money,'* were useless as it was
not the custom of the place to sell on credit. Every one who purchased
expected to pay. They were parted with, and the inscription now
stood, 'John Thompson sells hats.' 'Sells hats' says his next friend?
Why nobody will expect you to give them away. What then is the use
of that word? It was stricken out, and 'hats' followed it,—the rather
as there was one painted on the board. So his inscription was reduced
ultimately to 'John Thompson' with the figure of a hat subjoined."

249.   The Doctor told me at Paris, the two following anecdotes
of Abbe Raynal. He had a party to dine with him one day at Passy
of whom one half were Americans, the other half French and among
the last was the Abbe. During the dinner he got on his favorite theory
of the degeneracy of animals and even of man, in America, and urged
it with his usual eloquence. The Doctor at length noticing the acci-
dental stature and positions of his guests, at table, "Come," says he,
"M. L'Abbe, let us try this question by the fact before us. We are
here one half Americans, and one half French, and it happens that
the Americans have placed themselves on one side of the table, and
our French friends are on the other. Let both parties rise and we will
see on which side nature has degenerated." It happened that his
American guests were [William] Carmichael, Harmer [Josiah Harmar],
[David] Humphreys and others of the finest stature and form, while
those of the other side were remarkably diminutive, and the Abbe
himself particularly was a mere shrimp. He parried the appeal however, by a complimentary admission of exceptions, among which the
Doctor himself was a conspicuous one.

250.   The Doctor and Silas Deane were in conversation one day
at Passy on the numerous errors in the Abbe's *Histoire des deux Indes*,
when he happened to step in. After the usual salutations, Silas Deane
said to him "The Doctor and myself Abbe, were just speaking of the
errors of fact into which you have been led in your history." "Oh no,
Sir," said the Abbe, "that is impossible. I took the greatest care not
to insert a single fact, for which I had not the most unquestionable
authority." "Why," says Deane, "there is the story of Polly Baker,
and the eloquent apology you have put into her mouth, when brought
before a court of Massachusetts to suffer punishment under a law,
which you cite, for having had a bastard. I know there never was
such a law in Massachusetts." "Be assured," said the Abbe, "you are
mistaken, and that that is a true story. I do not immediately recollect
indeed the particular information on which I quote it, but I am certain that I had for it unquestionable authority." Doctor Franklin who
ha been for some time shaking with restrained laughter at the Abbe's
confidence in his authority for that tale, said, "I will tell you, Abbe,
the origin of that story. When I was a printer and editor of a newspaper, we were sometimes slack of news, and to amuse our customers,
I used to fill up our vacant columns with anecdotes, and fables, and
fancies of my own, and this of Polly Baker is a story of my making,
on one of those occasions." The Abbe without the least disconcert,
exclaimed with a laugh, "Oh, very well, Doctor, I had rather relate
your stories than other men's truths."

> Variant of *141*. TJ told this to a British visitor in 1817 (Francis
> Hall, *Travels in Canada and the United States* [1818], pp. 382–383).

 The next five anecdotes are from James Madison's "De-
tatched Memoranda," written within a few years of his
retirement in 1817, placed here for their connection with
those by Jefferson. Our text is from the edition by Elizabeth Fleet, *William and Mary Quarterly*, 3 ser., 3 (1946):
536–540, where they are prefaced with Madison's note:
"I did not become acquainted with Dr. Franklin till after
his return from France and election to the Chief Magis-
tracy of Pennsylvania. During the Session of the Grand
Convention, of which he was a member and as long after
as he lived, I had opportunities of enjoying much of his
conversation, which was always a feast to me. I never

passed half an hour in his company without hearing some observation or anicdote worth remembering. Among those which I have often repeated, and can therefore be sure that my memory accurately retains, are the following:"

251.   Previous to the Convention, and whilst the States were seeking by their respective regulations, to enlarge as much as possible their share of the general commerce, the Doctor alluding to their jealousies and competitions remarked that it would be best for all of them to let the trade be free, in which case it would level itself, and leave to each its proper share. These contests he said, put him in mind of what had once passed between a little boy and little girl eating milk and bread out of the same bowl, "Brother," cried the little girl, "eat on your side, you get more than your share."

252.   In the Convention, the difference of opinions was often very great, and it occasionally happened that the votes of the States were equally divided, and the questions undecided. On a particular day, when several subjects of great importance were successively discussed, and great diversity of opinions expressed, it happened that on each of them this was the case; so that nothing was done through the whole day and appearances were not a little discouraging, as to a successful issue to the undertaking. After the adjournment, the Doctor observed to several of us who were near him in allusion to the poor sample which had been given, of human reason that there was on board a ship in which he once crossed the Atlantic, a man who had from his birth been without the sense of smelling. On sitting down to dinner one day one of the men, cut off a piece of beef, and putting it to his nose cried out, this beef stinks. The one next to him, cutting and smelling a piece, said not at all, it is as sweet as any meat I ever smelt. A third passing a piece across his nose several times; stinks, says he, no, I believe not: yes, I believe it does, repeating the opposite opinions as often as he made the trial. The same doubts and contrarieties went round as the company, one after the other, expressed their opinions. Now, gentlemen, exclaimed the man, without the sense of smelling, I am satisfied of what I have long suspected, that what you call smelling has no existence, and that it is nothing but mere fancy and prejudice.

253.   In a conversation with him one day whilst he was confined

to his bed, the subject of religion with its various do[c]trines and modes happening to turn up, the Doctor remarked that he should be glad to see an experiment made of a religion that admitted of no pardon for transgressions; the hope of impunity being the great encouragement to them. In illustration of this tendency, he said that when he was a young man he was much subject to fits of indigestion brought on by indulgence at the table. On complaining of it to a friend, he recommended as a remedy a few drops of oil of wormwood, whenever that happened; and that he should carry a little viol of it about him. On trial he said he found the remedy to answer, and then said he, having my absolution in my pocket, I went on sinning more freely than ever.

254.   On entering his chamber in his extreme age when he had been much exhausted by pain and was particularly sensible of his weakness, Mr. Madison said he, these machines of ours however admirably formed will not last always. Mine I find is just worn out. It must have been an uncommonly good one I observed to last so long, especially under the painful malady which had co-operated with age in preying on it; adding that I could not but hope that he was yet to remain some time with us, and that the cause of his suffering might wear out faster than his Constitution. The only alleviation he said to his pain was opium, and that he found as yet to be a pretty sure one. I told him I took for granted he used it as sparingly as possible as frequent doses might otherwise impair his constitutional strength. He was well aware he said that every Dose he took had that effect; but he had no other remedy; and thought the best terms he could make with his complaint was to give up a part of his remaining life, for the greater ease of the rest.

> Following this anecdote, Madison wrote: "The following anecdotes are from the report of others." These are 255 and a repetition of 245.

255.   Among the measures of the first Revolutionary Congress, it was proposed that a Committee should be appointed to provide a Medical Chest for the army. The Doctor voted against it. Much surprize being manifested by some members, the Doctor in his justification, related an anecdote of the Celebrated Dr. [John] Fothergill, who being desired by a philosophical friend to say candidly whether he thought Physicians of real service to mankind, replied by observing

that he must first know whether his friend included old women among Physicians; If he did he thought they were of great service.

> Variant of *244*.

256.   "My dear Franklin," Mme. Helvétius said, "I hope you are happy." "I am happier every day," he replied. "I have never been so unfortunate as to be ill. Poor, then rich, I have always been content with what I have, never worrying about what I have not. But since growing older, since my passions have dimmed, I feel a peace of mind and heart that I never felt before, that these young people cannot know," he said, pointing to [Pierre] Cabanis and me. "At their age, the soul is *exterior*; at mine, *interior*—it looks out upon the noisy passersby without becoming involved in their quarrels."

> Letter by Constantine Volney, the historian, who lived for a time in the Helvétius home when BF was a frequent visitor; translated from Jean François Bodin, *Recherches Historiques sur l'Anjou*, 2 vols. (1821–1823), 2:436.

257.   [Elkanah Watson's] last interview with Franklin, who was then eighty years of age, had occurred in 1786. "On my first entering the room," Mr. Watson says, "he observed that all his old friends were dead, and he found himself alone, in the midst of a new generation, and added the remark, alike characteristic of the man and the philosopher, 'he was in their way, and it was time he was off the stage.'"

> Memoirs of Elkanah Watson, who, in 1780, had carried money to BF from Rhode Island, then remained in France as a prosperous merchant for several years; ed. W. C. Watson, *Men and Times of the Revolution* (1856), pp. 286–287.

258.   Who does not sympathize with the playful wish of the benign sage and devoted patriot Franklin, who, when he saw a little fly escape from a bottle in which it had been imprisoned, exclaimed, "I wish I could be corked up as you have been, and let out a hundred years hence, just to see how my dear America is going on"?

> Frances Wright, *Views and Manners in America* (1821), ed. P. R. Baker (1963), p. 63. Variant of 26. This variant may well have been a standing joke with BF, for it appears also in a letter by Samuel Petrie, 9 August 1796: "I remember one day at Dinner, with Doctor Franklin at Passy, in the Year 1779, the Doctor

produced a Fly, which had come out of a But of Madeira that Morning, and which by laying in the Sun was restored to Life.— The Doctor wish'd, that he cou'd, in like Manner, be bung'd up for fifty Years, and then restored to Life, to behold the flourishing State, in which America wou'd then be" (Joel J. Gold, "Dinner at Doctor Franklin's," *Modern Philology*, 75 [1978]: 391).

259.   I saw him try the experiment of flattening waves with oil, which had been regarded as a fable in Aristotle and Pliny. It is true they were not waves of the sea, but of a little stream that ran through the park at Wycombe. It was agitated by a tolerably fresh breeze. He went about two hundred paces from where we were, and after some magic grimaces, shook three times over the water, a reed, which he held in his hand. A moment after, the little waves began to grow smaller, and the surface of the water soon became smooth as glass.

260.   Franklin was very fond of Scotch songs, and often remembered the powerful and gentle emotions he had received from them. He related to us, that in travelling in America he met, beyond the Alleghany mountains, with the habitation of a Scotsman, living far from society, on account of the loss of his fortune, with his wife, who had been handsome, and a daughter of 15 or 16 years old; and that in a fine evening, seated in front of their door, the woman sung the Scotch air, "so merry as we have been," in so soft and touching a manner, that he melted into tears, and that this impression was still vivid in his mind after thirty years.

> Translated from *Mémoires Inedites de l'Abbé Morellet . . .*, 2 vols. (1821), 1:202–203, 298. Morellet dates the episode in 259 the end of April 1772, a time when BF liked to amuse his friends in this way, carrying "a little Oil in the upper hollow joint of my bamboo Cane" to use whenever the opportunity came (P 20:466). The next episode, however, seems fanciful since BF did not go beyond the Alleghenies.

261.   I was in France . . . and, speaking with Dr. Franklin of this singular disposition of men to quarrel and divide into parties, he gave his sentiments as usual by way of Apologue. He mentioned the Eddystone lighthouse in the British channel as being built on a rock in the mid-channel, totally inaccessible in winter, from the boisterous character of that sea, in that seaon. That therefore, for the two keepers employed to keep up the lights, all provisions for the winter were necessarily carried to them in autumn, as they could never be

visited again till the return of the milder season. That on the first practicable day in the spring a boat put off to them with fresh supplies. The boatmen met at the door one of the keepers and accosted him with a How goes it friend? Very well. How is your companion? I do not know. Don't know? Is not he here? I can't tell. Have not you seen him to-day? No. When did you see him? Not since last fall. You have killed him? Not I, indeed. They were about to lay hold of him, as having certainly murdered his companion; but he desired them to go up stairs and examine for themselves. They went up, and there found the other keeper. They had quarrelled it seems soon after being left there, had divided into two parties, assigned the cares below to one, and those above to the other, and had never spoken to or seen one another since.

> Thomas Jefferson's "Autobiography," *Writings of TJ*, ed. P. L. Ford, 10 vols. (1899), 1:76–77.

262.   While Franklin was negotiating in Paris, he sometimes went into a café to play at chess. A crowd usually assembled, of course to see the man rather than the play. Upon one occasion, Franklin lost in the middle of the game, when composedly taking the king from the board, he put him in his pocket, and continued to move. The antagonist looked up. The face of Franklin was so grave, and his gesture so much in earnest, that he began with an expostulatory, "Sir." "Yes, Sir, continue," said Franklin, "and we shall soon see that the party without a king will win the game."

> Letter by Frances Wright in America, relaying the anecdote from Lafayette, to Jeremy Bentham, 12 September 1821, ed. John Bowring, *Works of Jeremy Bentham*, 11 vols. (1838–1842), 10:527.

263.   Wit was an early characteristic of Franklin, and traits of it, that should have been considered mere marks of a sprightly mind, were regarded by many as the evidence of a perverse heart. The instance of his suggesting to his father, when engaged in packing a barrel of beef for winter's use, that *it would be a great saving of time, if instead of a long grace every day, over each piece he should ask a blessing over the whole at once,* was one of those graceless effusions, among others, that left a strong tinge of prejudice against him in the minds of his austere connections.

> William Tudor, *Life of James Otis* (1823), p. 388n. Variant of *151*.

264.   [Plaster of Paris] has even been introduced into America, where it was made known by Franklin upon his return from Paris. As this celebrated philosopher wished that the effects of this manure should strike the gaze of all cultivators, he wrote in great letters, formed by the use of the ground plaster, in a field of clover lying upon the great road to Washington, "This has been plastered." The prodigious vegetation which was developed in the plastered portion led him to adopt this method. Volumes upon the excellences of plaster would not have produced so speedy a revolution.

> John Antony Chaptal, *Chymistry Applied to Agriculture* (Paris, 1823; trans. Boston, 1839), p. 73. Introduced before the Revolution, plaster of Paris had become a favored fertilizer in Pennsylvania even before BF returned from Paris in 1785 (P. W. Bidwell and J. I. Falconer, *History of Agriculture* [1925], pp. 88–89).

265.   Franklin appeared at court in the dress of an American farmer. His straight unpowdered hair, his round hat, his brown cloth coat, formed a contrast with the laced and embroidered coats and the powdered and perfumed heads of the courtiers of Versailles. This novelty turned the enthusiastic heads of the French women. Elegant entertainments were given to Doctor Franklin, who to the reputation of a most skilful natural philosopher added the patriotic virtues which had invested him with the noble character of an apostle of liberty. I was present at one of these entertainments, when the most beautiful woman out of three hundred was selected to place a crown of laurels upon the white head of the American philosopher, and two kisses upon his cheeks.

> Jeanne Campan, *Memoirs of the Private Life of Marie Antoinette*, 2 vols. (1823; trans. 1917), 1:210. The story was vigorously denied by BF's secretary John Vaughan (Joshua Francis Fisher, *Recollections* [1929], p. 256).

266.   [Edward Rutledge] always a free talker upon revolutionary topics, was accustomed to relate an anecdote of Dr. Franklin, very characteristic of that extraordinary man, and which does not appear to have been elsewhere noticed.

Upon taking leave of Lord Howe, his lordship politely sent the commissioners to New York in his own barge, and just as they were approaching the shore, the doctor began to chink some gold and silver coin in his breeches pocket, of which, upon their arrival at the wharf, he very formally offered a handful to the sailors who had rowed the boat. The commanding officer, not permitting them to accept the money, the doctor very deliberately replaced it in his pocket: when questioned by his associates upon so unexpected a procedure, he observed, "As these people are under the impression that we have not a farthing of hard money in the country, I thought I would convince them of their mistake; I knew, at the same time, that I risked nothing by an offer which their regulations and discipline would not permit them to accept."

> The biographical sketch of Edward Rutledge, probably by Arthur Middleton, in John Sanderson, *Biography of the Signers of the Declaration of Independence*, 9 vols (1823–1827), 3:25–26. For anecdotes related to the mission of BF, John Adams, and Rutledge in 1776, see *79* and *199*.

 The next four anecdotes have been translated from Pierre Cabanis, *Œuvres Posthumes*, 5 vols. (1825), vol. 5. A young medical student, Cabanis was virtually an adopted son of Mme Helvétius during the time that BF frequented her home.

267.   After reading a tract on "The Custom of Eating Meat," Franklin remained convinced of the barbarity and pernicious effects of this custom, and resolved never to eat anything that once had life. [*Note:* In the first part of his *Memoirs*, Franklin said this idea and the resolution he made had come from reading an article of (Thomas) Tryon's on the same subject. But we have heard him tell it as we report it here.]

His mother let him go on, persuaded that the fantasy would not last. Nevertheless, she soon saw she was mistaken; and when a friend asked who had put such a thing into her son's head, she replied: "Some fool of a philosopher"—adding in a whisper, "It is not so bad; it teaches him self-control. He is learning that you can do anything if your will is strong enough."

> Page 225. Variant of *133*.

268.   One day after talking about [practical virtue], he concluded by telling us, in his French, the weakness of which added even

more grace and force: If villains understood the advantages of being virtuous, they would turn honest out of villainy.

Page 230.

269.   Franklin read [in the Proverbs of Solomon] length of days is in your right hand and fortune in your left. This was a ray of light for him: So that is how a man lives long and acquires the wealth he needs for happiness! He vowed to follow that proverb by example, on one point or another. He was 20 at the time, and at 80 he told us about it, adding: "See for yourself whether I was right. My health has never been better than it is today. I have, not affluence, but enough for my needs. And the world knows well enough that King George came off badly in his quarrels with that printer fellow."

Page 231. BF kept *Proverbs* 3:16–17 in his notebook (NCE p. 355).

270.   He said that when dealing with politicians he was careful to speak the exact truth: "That is my only cunning. Politicians are so corrupt that I always fool them this way."

Page 248.

271.   When Dr. Franklin was in Scotland, he often met with [David] Hume. One day, when the Doctor was detailing the natural advantages of America, and prophesying what a country it would become, "You have forgotten one little article, Doctor," said David, "among your projected manufactures, the manufacture of men"; the increase of population in America has verified this prophesy.

Henry Mackenzie, *Anecdotes and Egotisms* (1825), ed. H. W. Thompson (1927), p. 170. For BF's remark on manufacturing men, see above, 79n.

272.   The commissioners [seeking French aid in 1777] had assembled at Dr. Franklin's apartments on the rumor that a special messenger had arrived and were too impatient to suffer a moment's delay. They received him in the court yard. Before he had time to alight Dr. Franklin addressed him. Sir, is Philadelphia taken? Yes sir. The old gentleman clasped his hands and returned to the hotel. But, sir, I have greater news than that—*General Burgoyne and his whole army are prisoners of war!* The effect was electrical. The despatches

were scarcely read before they were put under copy. Mr. [Jonathan Loring] Austin was himself impressed into the service of transcribing them. . . . Dr. Franklin transferred to Mr. Austin the affection of a father, as if he had been not merely the messenger, but the cause of this glorious information. He took him directly into his family, constituted him an additional private secretary, and continued towards him the kindest regards during the whole period of his remaining in France. Often at breakfast or other occasions of their meeting, the old gentleman would break from one of those musings in which it was his habit to indulge, and clasping his hands together exclaim, Oh! Mr. Austin, you brought us glorious news!

273.   Among numberless similar instances of the consideration in which he was held, a large cake was sent one morning to the commissioners' apartment inscribed "Le digne Franklin." [*Note:* "For the worthy Franklin."] We have, said one of the gentlemen, as usual to thank you for our accommodations and to appropriate your present to our joint use. Not at all, said the Doctor, this must be intended for all the commissioners, only these French people cannot write English. They mean no doubt Lee, Dean, Franklin. That might answer said Mr. [Arthur] Lee, but we know whenever they remember us at all, they always put you first.

> "Memoir of Jonathan Loring Austin," *Boston Monthly Magazine,* 2 (July 1826): 59, 60–61. S. E. Morison's sketch of Austin in the *DAB* says this "highly imaginative" memoir was by J. T. Austin.

274.   Whilst the last members were signing [the Constitution] Doctor Franklin looking towards the Presidents Chair, at the back of which a rising sun happened to be painted, observed to a few members near him, that Painters had found it difficult to distinguish in their art a rising from a setting sun. . . . But now at length I have the happiness to know it is a rising and not a setting Sun.

> *The Debates . . . Reported by James Madison,* ed. G. Hunt and J. B. Scott (1920), p. 583, facing a photocopy of the ms. A variant of *144.*

275.   The Doctor was walking one day in Front street, near Chesnut street, in the city of Philadelphia, at the dawn of our Revolution, when he was thus accosted by a Tar:—

"Is your name Ben Franklin?" Yes. "Are you the man who invented saw-dust pudding?" Yes, replied the Doctor. "Then," said the sailor, "for God's sake don't give the receipt to make it to old F*****, our merchant, as he will feed all his crews on it."

276.   The story of the saw-dust pudding *alter dictum*, wheat bran pudding arose in this manner. The Doctor had conducted an independent paper in Philadelphia, which gave offence to a class who wanted to rule every body in their own way, and the heads of this party, some fifteen or twenty, informed the Doctor that they would frown him down, unless he would submit to the curb. The Doctor proposed to explain, and fixed the time at his own house where the gentlemen were invited to dine. He requested his lady to employ two pence in the purchase of a peck of wheat bran, and to make two puddings of it— one for each end of the table, as he was to have fifteen or twenty friends to dine with him.— The company met— the two puddings were served on table, without any other dishes— the company sat down, and each friend was served with his slice of pudding. Their curiosity led them to try it— they examined each other's countenance, and at length were satiated with the pudding. Friends, says the Doctor, will you be helped to more? No, they all replied, we have enough of your pudding. But what means this? Why, replied the Doctor, it means to tell you that these two puddings cost two pence, and fifteen friends say they have enough.— Know then, that as long as Benjamin Franklin can satisfy fifteen friends with two pence, he never will sacrifice the independence of his paper.

The Casket, or Flowers of Literature, Wit and Sentiment, 1 (May 1827): 191. For variants, see 216 and 283.

277.   Dr. Franklin was once a member of a body in which it was contended that a certain amount of property, (fifty dollars we think) should be required for voting. The doctor was opposed to it. "Today," said he, "a man owns a jackass worth fifty dollars, and he is entitled to vote; but before the next election the jackass dies. The man in the mean time, has become more experienced, his knowledge of the principles of government, and his acquaintance with mankind, are more extensive, and he is therefore better qualified to make a proper selection of rulers— But the jackass is dead and the man cannot vote. Now, gentlemen," said he, addressing himself to the

advocates of that qualification,— "pray inform me, in whom is the right of suffrage? In the man or in the jackass?"

The Casket, or Flowers of Literature, Wit and Sentiment, 4 (April 1828):181.

 The next five anecdotes are in the notebooks of Robert Gilmor, a bon vivant and autograph collector, with this prefatory note: "The following anecdotes of Dr. Franklin were communicated to me by Charles Carroll of Carroll-ton, Esq., the present [1828] survivor of the signers of the Declaration of Independence." Our text is from "The Album of Robert Gilmor of Baltimore," ed. F. L. Plead-well, *American Collector,* 6 (1928):22–23.

278.   It is well known that at the commencement of our Revolution, a Committee of Congress, consisting of Dr. Franklin, Samuel Chase, and Mr. Carroll (from whom I had the story) was appointed to go to Canada with a view to sound the disposition of that colony for revolt. Dr. [John] Carroll, afterwards Archbishop of Baltimore, was added to the Committee to operate on the Catholic population. The mission failed in its object and considerable apprehension was entertained of ill treatment before the members of it could escape from the country. Dr. Franklin, regardless of his own safety, was very solicitous about that of his colleagues, and urged Mr. Carroll to get away as fast as he could, saying, "You and Chase are young men, and can get off readily, but as I am an old man, I shall only embarrass you; therefore leave me to my fate."

279.   Mr. Carroll once asked Dr. Franklin what had become of the millions of francs *deficient* of the three millions granted by the King of France and which had been supposed by some to have been appropriated by the Doctor to his own use. He replied that he had himself asked the same question of the Count de Vergennes, who answered very pettishly, that the Doctor knew very well the whole was a free gift of the King, and that it did not become those who received it to question the accuracy of the account.

280.   Samuel Chase, his colleague in the mission to Canada (afterwards Judge Chase), was a man of very loose and free conversation, and a great epicure. When Mr. Carroll was in the Senate in

Philadelphia, he went to see Dr. Franklin, and in the course of conversation, the Doctor suddenly asked, "How's Chase? Does he talk as much of girls and oysters as he used to do?"

281.   A short time before Franklin's death Mr. Carroll went to see him and found him confined to his couch. He pressed Mr. Carroll to dine with him, observing at the same time, "I cannot *sit with you* at table, but I can *see* you." He was obliged to lie in a recumbent position.

282.   Congress was in session in Philadelphia when information was brought of the Doctor's death. Mr. Carroll rose in his place and moved that the Senate should go into mourning for so distinguished a patriot. He was seconded. [*Note:* In conversing again with Mr. Carroll on this subject, he says he was seconded by the Senator from Philadelphia, but none but themselves voted in the affirmative. He is of opinion that the dislike felt by Ralph Izard was occasioned by his being in the background in France, when he and Arthur Lee were there, with Franklin who commanded the respect and admiration of the whole court, and left his associates unnoticed.] When he sat down Ralph Izard of South Carolina came round to his chair and said, "Why, Carroll, what's got into you, to think of voting honours to that d——d old rascal?"

 The next four anecdotes are from John F. Watson, *Annals of Philadelphia*, (1830), pp. 513–515.

283.   Not long after Benjamin Franklin had commenced editor of a newspaper, he noticed with considerable freedom the public conduct of one or two influential persons in Philadelphia. This circumstance was regarded by some of his patrons with disapprobation, and induced one of them to convey to Franklin the opinion of his friends in regard to it. The Doctor listened with patience to the reproof, and begged the favor of his friend's company at supper on an evening which he named; at the same time requesting that the other gentlemen who were dissatisfied with him should also attend. The invitation was accepted by Philip Syng, Hugh Roberts, and several others. The Doctor received them cordially, and his editorial conduct was canvassed, and some advice given. Supper was at last announced, and the guests invited to an adjoining room. The Doctor begged the

party to be seated, and urged them to help themselves; but the table was only supplied with *two puddings and a stone pitcher filled with water!* Each guest had a plate, a spoon, and a penny porringer; they were all helped; but none but the Doctor could eat; he partook freely of the pudding, and urged his friends to do the same; but it was out of the question— they tasted and tried in vain. When their facetious host saw the difficulty was unconquerable, he rose and addressed them thus: "My friends, any one who can subsist upon saw-dust pudding and water, as I can, needs no man's patronage!"

> Variant of 216 and 277; many variants which also obscured the point that "sawdust pudding" was bran pudding appeared down to our own time; for example, Thomas Fleming, *The Man Who Dared the Lightning* (1971), p. 18.

284.   Edward Duffield . . . told me that Franklin told his father, that when he was in France, and travelling, he sometimes made a temporary Æolian harp by stretching a silken cord across some crevice where air passed. On one such occasion in repassing such a house after an elapse of years, he found it deserted because of their hearing strange but melodious sounds, which they deemed good evidence of its being haunted. On entering the house he found vestiges of the silk remaining—the creator of all the mischief!

285.   He once told Dr. [George] Logan that the celebrated Adam Smith, when writing his "Wealth of Nations," was in the habit of bringing chapter after chapter as he composed it, to himself, Dr. [Richard] Price and others of the literati; then patiently hear their observations, and profit by their discussions and criticism— even sometimes submitting to write whole chapters anew, and even to reverse some of his propositions.

286.   My aged friend, Samuel Preston, tells me some anecdotes of Dr. Franklin when he was at the Indian treaty at Easton in 1756. Preston's father, then there, much admired Franklin's ready wit. When the old Indians came in their file to speak to the Governor [Robert Hunter Morris] he would ask their names; then the Governor would ask Ben, as he called him, what he must think of to remember them by. He was always answered promptly. At last one Indian came whose name was Tocarededhogan. Such a name! How shall it be remembered? The answer was prompt:— Think of a wheelbarrow—to carry a dead hog on.

287.   While he was Ambassador to the English court, a lady, who was about to be presented to the king, noticed his exceedingly plain appearance, and inquired who he was. "That, madam," answered the gentleman on whose arm she was leaning, "is Benjamin Franklin, the Ambassador from North America." "The North American Ambassador, so shabbily dressed!" exclaimed the lady. "Hush, madam, for heaven's sake," whispered the gentleman, "he is the man that bottles up thunder and lightning."

288.   "Friend Franklin," said Myers Fisher, the celebrated Quaker lawyer of Philadelphia, one day, to the Doctor, "thee knows almost every thing: can thee tell me how I am to preserve my small beer in the back yard? My neighbors are often tapping it of nights." "Put a barrel of old Madeira by the side of it," replied the Doctor— "let them but get a taste of the Madeira, and I will engage that they will never trouble the small beer any more."

> Freeman Hunt, *American Anecdotes*, 2 vols. (1830), 1:36–37. The second anecdote, 288, is an old jestbook favorite: In the *American Jest Book* (1789) it is told about a nameless butler who, when asked by his mistress how a cask of excellent small beer could be preserved, replied, "By placing a barrel of good ale by it" (pp. 33–34).

289.   Dr. Franklin, with a party of his friends, was overtaken by bad weather on one of the West Indian islands (which they had put into on a voyage to Europe), and took shelter in a public house, kept by a foreigner. Upon their requesting that more wood might be brought and put on the fire, the inhuman brute of a landlord ordered his sickly wife to go out in the storm and bring it! while a young sturdy negro wench stood by doing nothing! When asked, why he did not send the girl, rather than his wife, he replied, "That wench is worth £80, and if she should catch cold, and die, it would be a great loss to me; but, if my wife dies, I can get another, and perhaps money into the bargain."

> *Percy Anecdotes*, rev. ed., 2 vols. (New York, 1834), 2:78. BF voyaged four times to Europe, but never mentioned putting into the West Indian islands.

290.   "We must be unanimous," observed [John] Hancock, on the occasion of signing the Declaration of Independence; "there must

be no pulling different ways; we must all hang together." "Yes," added Franklin, "we must all hang together, or most assuredly we shall all *hang separately.*"

> *American Joe Miller* (1839), p. 181. As recently as 1830, this was being told as though Richard Penn had made the pun (Freeman Hunt, *American Anecdotes*, 2:97), but Jared Sparks reprinted the present version in 1840 (*Works of BF*, 1:408), and, despite the strong disclaimer by Carl Van Doren in 1938 (*BF*, pp. 551–552), the story lives on as BF's in current dictionaries of quotations.

291.   In the habitual innocency and playfulness which he was fond of indulging with his grandchildren, he frequently introduced, in reproof of too light and frequent volubility, this admonition:— "Recollect you have two ears, and two eyes, and only one mouth, which shows you must not speak more than half what you hear, and of half as much as you see."

> Preface to William Duane, ed., *Memoirs of BF*, 2 vols. (1834–1840), 1:xxxiv.

292.   The Minister of the United States made his appearance, followed by a gigantic warrior in the garb of his native woods. . . .

"I was waiting for you, sir," the King said peevishly, in spite of the alarmed pressure which the Queen gave his royal arm. . . . "I wished to— to say farewell to Tatua before his departure," said Louis XVI, looking rather awkward. "Approach, Tatua." And the gigantic Indian strode up, and stood undaunted before the magistrate of the French nation. . . .

A smile played around Doctor Franklin's lips, as he whittled his cane with more vigor than ever.

"I believe, your excellency, Tatua has done good service elsewhere than at Quebec," the King said, appealing to the American envoy; "at Bunker's Hill, at Brandywine, at York Island? Now that Lafayette and my brave Frenchmen are among you, your excellency need have no fear but that the war will finish quickly. They will teach you discipline, and the way to conquer."

"King Louis of France," said the envoy, clapping his hat down over his head, and putting his arms a-kimbo, "we have learned that from the British, to whom we are superior in every thing: and I'd have your majesty to know, that in the art of whipping the world we have no need of any French lessons. If your reglars jines General Washington, 'tis to larn from him how Britishers are licked, for I'm blest if yu know the way yet."

Tatua said, "Ugh," and gave a rattle with the butt of his carbine, which made the timid monarch start; the eyes of the lovely Antoinette flashed fire, but it played round the head of the dauntless American envoy harmless as the lightning which he knew how to conjure away.

> Ladies Repository (Cincinnati), 8 (1848): 28–29, with a note warning that it is a "piece of satire, taken from an English print."

293.   At the time when the celebrated Dr. Franklin lay upon his death-bed, he was visited by a young man who had a great respect for his judgment in all things; and having entertained doubts as to the truth of the Scriptures, he thought that this awful period afforded a suitable opportunity of consulting the doctor on this important subject. Accordingly, he introduced it in a solemn and weighty manner, inquiring of Franklin what were his sentiments as to the truth of the Scriptures. On the question being put, although he was in a very weak state, and near his decease, he replied, "Young man, my advice to you is, that you cultivate an acquaintance with, and firm belief in, the Holy Scriptures: this is your certain interest."

> Kazlitt Arvine, Cyclopedia of Moral and Religious Anecdotes (1849), p. 55e.

294.   In relating the reminiscences of his apprenticeship, [Benjamin] Russell often spoke of Dr. Franklin, who passed through Worcester several times, and never failed to call at [Isaiah] Thomas's office, and hold some conversation with the workmen. "With several other young men (said Russell) I was out in the fields one day, when we were overtaken by a tremendous thunder-shower. Some of the party proposed to take shelter under a large tree— others proposed to go into a barn hard by. I objected to both, and advised that we should shelter ourselves under the projecting cliff of a large rock. My advice was followed. Both the tree and barn were struck by lightning, but the rock remained untouched. I mentioned this incident to Dr. Franklin, who patted me on the head, and asked if I was influenced in my judgement by what he had written. I replied that I was. The

Doctor smiled, pleasantly, and ever afterwards recognized me when he visited our office."

Joseph T. Buckingham, *Specimens of Newspaper Literature*, 2 vols. (1850), 2:8-9.

295.   My grandfather had sold a swift Narragansett black mare, which he and the family had often rode to the house of his friend; and this horse came into the possession of Dr. Franklin, who, in one of his journeys to Boston, came unconsciously opposite to the lane leading to the house of Mr. Eells. . . . The horse instantly wheeled towards the house, and the rider applied whip and spur and voice in vain to force the animal along the public road. At length he gave her the rein, and away she flew for the house, and was soon at the door. The family, seeing a strange gentleman ride up, soon lined the windows; and the reverend gentleman coming out made a courteous bow to the traveller, as if to bid him welcome. He raised his hat in turn, and added, "Sir, my name is Benjamin Franklin, of Philadelphia. I am travelling to Boston, and my horse appears to have some business with you, as he has insisted upon coming to your house." "Oh, sir," replied Mr. Eells, "that horse has often been here before. Pray alight and come in and lodge with us tonight." . . . He used to remark that he believed he was the only man who was ever introduced by his horse. This anecdote I had from my mother.

Autobiography of Benjamin Silliman, composed after his retirement from Yale in 1853; *Life of Benjamin Silliman*, ed. G. P. Fisher, 2 vols. (1866), 1:12-13.

296.   One fine morning, when Franklin was busy preparing his newspaper for the press, a lounger stepped into the store, and spent an hour or more looking over the books, etc., and finally, taking one in his hand, asked the shop boy the price.

"One dollar," was the answer.

"One," said the lounger, "can't you take less than that?"

"No, indeed, one dollar is the price."

Another hour had nearly passed, when the lounger asked, "Is Mr. Franklin at home?"

"Yes, he is in the printing office."

"I want to see him," said the lounger.

The shop boy immediately informed Mr. Franklin that a

gentleman was in the store wanting to see him. Franklin was soon behind the counter, when the lounger, with book in hand, addressed him thus: "Mr. Franklin, what is the lowest you can take for this book?"

"One dollar and a quarter," was the ready answer.

"One dollar and a quarter? Why, your young man asked only a dollar."

"True, said Franklin, "and I could have better afforded to have taken a dollar then, than to have been taken out of the office."

The lounger seemed surprised, and wishing to end the parley of his own making, said, "Come, Mr. Franklin, tell me what is the lowest you can take for it."

"One dollar and a half."

"One dollar and a half? Why, you offered it yourself for a dollar and a quarter."

"Yes," said Franklin, "and I had better have taken that price then, than a dollar and a half now."

The lounger paid down the price, and went about his business—if he had any—and Franklin returned into the printing office.

> Home Magazine, 3 (January 1854):23, and two years later in its children's section, 7 (January 1856): 20.

297.   Miss Elizabeth Shewell became acquainted with Benjamin West, afterwards the celebrated artist, and they fell in love with each other. West at that time, although descended from a good family, was poor and little known. Stephen Shewell wished his sister to marry another suitor, which she refused to do, in consequence of her attachment to West. The brother objected to West on account of his poverty and obscurity, and he was forbidden to come to the house. Miss Shewell, however, continued to see him elsewhere, and they became engaged to be married. West then determined to go to Europe and prosecute his studies and profession there, and Miss Shewell promised him that when he notified her of his ability to maintain her and of his wish for her to come to him, she would proceed to join him in any part of Europe and marry him. Her brother was informed of her meetings with West, and of the engagements she had entered into with him; so to prevent any further intercourse between them he confined her to her chamber and kept her under lock and key until after West's departure for Europe.

West pursued his studies and profession for some time in various places on the Continent, and finally settled at London, where he soon met with sufficient patronage to justify him in calling on Miss Shewell to fulfill her promise. He then made arrangements for her to come to him in the same vessel that conveyed his request to her, and also that his father should accompany her on the voyage. Upon the receipt of his message, Miss Shewell prepared for her departure, but her brother was apprised of her intention, and again confined her to her chamber. Her engagement to West was well known in Philadelphia, and her brother's tyrannical treatment of her excited great indignation against him, and strong sympathy for his sister. In this state of things, the late Bishop [William] White, who was my guest on his last patriarchal visit to Easton, told us that he, (then about eighteen years of age) and Dr. Franklin, (about fifty-nine years of age) and Francis Hopkinson, (twenty-nine years of age) when the vessel was ready to sail, procured a rope ladder, went to the captain and engaged him to set sail as soon as they brought a lady on board; took old Mr. West to the ship, and went at midnight to Stephen Shewell's home, attached the ladder to a window in Miss Shewell's chamber, and got her safely out and to the vessel, which sailed a few minutes after she entered it.

> Letter by Joseph K. Swift to Horatio G. Jones, corresponding secretary of the Pennsylvania Historical Society, dated 1858, in George Smith, *History of Delaware County* (Philadelphia, 1862), p. 514. Ms Shewell eloped in 1764, but BF did not know the future Bishop White until 1770 (P 17:246). Still the story became popular, especially as rewritten by Rebecca Harding Davis, "Old Philadelphia," *Harper's New Monthly Magazine*, 52 (April 1876): 721, with BF as "the good angel." The whole story is discounted by Theodore Hornberger, "Mr. Hicks of Philadelphia," *Pennsylvania Magazine of History and Biography*, 53 (1929): 349–350.

298.   One evening in the apartment of Mme. de Chaumont, Franklin began a game of chess with a priest who served as tutor to the heir of the family. When the lady wished to retire, the game was transferred at Franklin's suggestion to his own quarters. There one game succeeded to another, until the supply of candles became exhausted. Franklin, absorbed by the pleasures of combat, protested, "My dear abbé, it is impossible for two men such as we to give up because of the lack of illumination." The priest thereupon offered to

seek a new supply of candles in his own quarters and set off with Franklin's benediction. "May the goddess of night protect you in your adventurous journey." In his absence Franklin took advantage of the last flickers of candlelight treacherously to plot a check-mate. He was still far from having arranged it when the abbé returned with a bewildered air. "What is wrong?" Franklin asked. "You look like a man who has just lost two chess-games. Has the goddess of night failed to answer my prayer or has Mercury sent one of his imps to our park?" "It is not at all matter of night and robbers," replied the abbé. "It is Phoebus or at least Aurora with her rosy fingers who reigns at this moment." So saying, he opened the blinds and the sunlight filled the room. "You are right, it is daytime," Franklin replied calmly. "Let's go to bed."

> Vincent le Ray de Chaumont, grandson of BF's landlord at Passy, *La Semaine des Familles*, 2 vols. (1859), 1:385–387; trans. A. O. Aldridge, *F and His French Contemporaries* (1957), pp. 196–197.

299.   The following anecdote was related to me, a few years ago, by a gentleman of this city [Philadelphia], who was a descendant of one of the founders of the Pennsylvania Hospital:

At the first meeting held to consider the establishment of the hospital, one of the persons present said that he was opposed to having any hospital; that the result would be that sick persons would come to Philadelphia from all the colonies, to be cured.

"If that should be the case," said Dr. Franklin, "we shall do more good than we expected."

> A correspondent, "M. E.," in the *Historical Magazine*, 5 (April 1861): 117. The hospital was founded in 1751.

 The next four anecdotes are from a letter by Colonel Robert Carr, dated 25 May 1864, in the *Historical Magazine*, n.s. 4 (August 1868): 59, 60. Colonel Carr, who died in 1866 aged ninety, prefaced his remarks as "only the crude reminiscence of a thoughtless school-boy of eleven or twelve years of age, whose opportunities of seeing the Doctor occurred from the fact of my residing near his house and being intimate with, and the playmates of, his two youngest grandsons."

300.   A court, or alley, ten feet wide, called "Franklin Court," extended from Market-street to the rear of the house, which was built with the front towards Chesnut-street; but, sometime after it was erected, it was discovered that the title to the front of the lot, on Chesnut-street, was defective; and the Doctor, rather than engage in a litigation, or pay an exorbitant price demanded by the claimant of the lot, abandoned it, and used the Market-street avenue.

301.   During the latter years of the Doctor's life, he was afflicted with the gout and stone. For the latter, his friends wished him to submit to an operation; but he said that at his age it was not worth while to undergo the pain. Although he suffered much from his afflictions, he was remarkably patient and mild. When able to be out of bed, he passed nearly all his time in his office, reading and writing, and in conversation with his friends; and, when the boys were playing and very noisy, in the lot front of the office, he would open the window and call to them: "Boys, Boys, can't you play without making so much noise. I am reading, and it disturbs me very much." I have heard the servants in his family say that he never used a hasty or angry word to any one.

302.   On one occasion, when his servant was absent, he called me into his office, to carry a letter to the Post-office. Whilst waiting for it, there was a candle burning on the table, with which he had been melting sealing-wax. He told me to put it out and set it away. I took up the candlestick and blew the candle out, when he said: "Stop, my boy, I will show you the right way to put out a candle. Light it again." Accordingly, I lighted the candle; and the Doctor lifted it out of the candlestick, turning the blazing end down, until the tallow had *nearly* extinguished it, when he quickly turned it up, and blew it out. "Now," said he, "it can be lighted again very readily; and the grease will not run down the candle."

303.   The Doctor was remarkable for always having some kind word of advice or encouragement, for those around him. You may recollect the anecdote, which has been published, of his conversation with the man, who was blacking his shoes: "John," said the Doctor, "I was once as poor a man as you; but I was industrious and saved my earnings, until now I have enough to enable me to live in comfort in my old age." "Ah, but Doctor," replied John, "if every one was as saving and as rich as you, who would black your shoes?"

304.   [William Franklin] was set one day to work an electrical machine on which his father was intending an experiment with a live duck. Inclining forward, and holding the creature's head towards the machine, it struggled violently to escape, and the experimentalist's head meeting the shock instead, he fell senseless to the floor, and was with great difficulty restored to animation.

> Letter by "E. L. S." in *Notes and Queries*, 4 ser., 4 (1869): 558, even mistaking "Temple" for "William" Franklin, and garbling the event in *176*.

305.   I [Ward Boylston] was introduced at his seat near Paris, in the year 1783. There were several gentlemen and ladies in the room at the time of my name being announced to him, when he arose from his chair and took me by the hand, saying, "I shall ever revere the name of Boylston; Sir, are you of the family of Dr. Zabdiel Boylston of Boston?" to which I replied that he was my great uncle; "then, Sir, I must tell you I owe everything I now am to him." He went on giving this account of himself, viz.: "When Dr. Boylston was in England, I was there reduced to the greatest distress, a youth without money, friends or counsel. I applied in my extreme distress to him, who supplied me with twenty guineas; and, relying, on his judgment, I visited him as opportunities offered, and by his fatherly counsels and encouragements I was saved from the abyss of destruction which awaited me, and my future fortune was based upon his parental advice and timely assistance."

> From Ward Nicholas Boylston's manuscript, ed. C. W. Parsons, "Zabdiel and John Boylston," *New England Historical and Genealogical Register*, 35 (1881):150–151. Zabdiel Boylston had been an adversary of James Franklin's *New-England Courant* in a controversy over vaccination in 1721. He was in London during 1724–1725 when BF was there, but I have found no other account of their meeting except in Arthur B. Tourtellot, *BF: The Shaping of Genius* (1977), p. 272, which is based on this anecdote.

306.   Félix Nogaret, an almanac poet, having translated Turgot's hexameter into French (Il ôte au ciel la foudre et le sceptre aux tyrans), sent it to Franklin with three pages of complimentary commentary. Franklin's reply may be thus translated: "Sir, I have received the letter in which, having overwhelmed me with a torrent of compliments I

regret not feeling worthy of, you ask my opinion of the translation of a Latin verse. I am too little of a connoisseur of the elegance and subtleties of your admirable language, to dare sit in judgment upon the poetry which is to be found in this verse. . . . I only wish you to notice two inexact expressions in the original. In spite of my experiments in electricity, the lightning still strikes our nose or our beard; and, so far as the tyrant is concerned, more than a million of us united to snatch his sceptre from him."

> Samuel Arthur Bent, *Familiar Short Sayings of Great Men* (1882, 1887), pp. 228–229. BF's original reply, 8 March 1781, said merely the Revolution had been the work of many able and brave men (Smyth 8:215); the added witticism could have derived from misreading James Parton's *Life and Times of BF*, 2 vols. (1864), where BF's letter is followed by a separate statement: "In more jocular moments he would say, that, as to the thunder, he left it where he found it, and that more than a million of his countrymen cooperated with him in snatching the sceptre" (2:434–435).

307.   Once he attended a memorable banquet in Paris shortly after the close of the Revolutionary War. Among the speakers was the English Ambassador, who responded to the toast, "Great Britain." The Ambassador dwelt at length on England's greatness and likened her to the sun that sheds its beneficent rays on all. The next toast was "America," and Franklin was called upon to respond. He began modestly by saying: "The Republic is too young to be spoken of in terms of praise; her career is yet to come, and so, instead of America, I will name you a man, George Washington—the Joshua who successfully commanded the sun to stand still." The Frenchmen at the board forgot the courtesy due their English guest, and laughed needlessly loud.

> Elbert Hubbard, *Little Journeys to the Homes of American Statesmen* (1898), pp. 67–68; a variant of 212.

308.   In one of his letters he imagines a man at the gates of heaven and applying for entrance on the ground that he was a Presbyterian. 'What is that?' St. Peter asked, and when told he answered, 'We don't have any here.' The astonished man mentioned different sects only to be rebuffed with the news that there were none of these persuasions in heaven. Finally, the man saw his wife through the gate and claimed that if she was there he should be too, for they were of

the same religion on earth. "Oh," said St. Peter, "why didn't you say that you were a Christian, to begin with?"

> P. L. Ford, *Many-Sided F* (1899), pp. 156–157; I have been unable to find this letter.

309.   Mistress Betty [Elizabeth Greene] positively and steadfastly refused all the Doctor's invitations for a horseback ride with him, though she owned one of the finest saddle horses in the county and was exceedingly fond of riding.

Her conduct became so marked that her father at last deemed it necessary to remonstrate with her. "My daughter," said he, "why do you persist in such discourtesy to Dr. Franklin? No one should treat a guest under his roof as you are treating him. . . ."

In those days children were brought up to obey their parents, even when they were no longer children. Mistress Betty dared not say "Nay" when Dr. Franklin proposed a ride to Providence a few days after. The saddle horses were brought to the door. The handsome old Doctor and the haughty Mistress Betty cantered out from under the elms planted by her great-grandfather, Deputy Governor John Greene, when he built the house 100 years before for her eldest son, her grandfather, upon his coming of age. . . . Tradition fails to tell what they talked about. . . . At least we know the good old Doctor's conversation was not entirely fatherly in its tone, for when they reached home, at the close of the day, Mistress Betty informed her honored father of the result of the day's outing in these words: "Don't you ever ask me to ride with that old fool again."

> A "true story" attributed to Miss Mary A. Greene in 1901, George Sears Greene, *The Greenes of Rhode Island*, ed. Louise Brownell Clarke (1903), pp. 169–170. Ms. Greene's memory is suspect, for she confuses dates and places BF in Rhode Island ten years too late.

310.   When the sessions [of the Constitutional Convention] were over, a lady asked Franklin: "Well, Doctor, what have we got, a republic or a monarchy?" "A republic," replied the doctor, "if you can keep it."

> Max Farrand, *Fathers of the Constitution* (1921), pp. 134–135; revitalized. in Alistair Cooke's television series, "America: a Personal History of the United States," 1972 (*Alistair Cooke's America* [1973], p. 136).

311.   He could not appear in any salon but what he was immediately surrounded by several beauties, and if he sat down, they sat down too—on the arms of his chair. Such eagerness at times caused him some difficulty, for each one wanted to be the most beloved. But like a sage, he had foreseen the possibility and turned it to advantage. When one them would ask if he didn't love her the most, he would always answer: "Yes, when you are the nearest to me, on account of the force of attraction."

> Bernard Faÿ, F, *the Apostle of Modern Times*, based on six hundred previously unpublished letters found in France (1929), p. 457.

312.   Soon after taking up residence [at Passy, early 1777], Franklin was visited by one of his neighbors, a fellow scientist and political philosopher, Jean Sylvain Bailly, who had taken him for a model and hoped to become a kind of French Franklin. After entering the salon, Bailly lapsed into silence, respectfully waiting for his host to begin the conversation. Eventually he offered Franklin a pinch of tobacco, which was refused. After two hours of silence, Bailly got up to leave—and Franklin's only words as he showed out his visitor were "fort bien." Bailly . . . frequently said that "fort bien" were the only words that he had ever heard from Franklin when no other company was present.

> A. O. Aldridge, BF, *Philosopher and Man* (1965), p. 271.

313.   Franklin was not in the least inhibited in stating his anti-blue blood opinions to the French aristocrats. One day he took on a whole roomful of them. Their spokesman insisted that the majority could not possibly rule in a state because they were uneducated and ill-informed. Only the educated and well-informed minority should govern. Finally the nobleman attempted to trump Franklin by appealing to others in the room. He asked all those who agreed with him to rise. Everyone stood up, leaving Franklin alone in his chair. Totally unabashed, he declared himself the winner. "According to your own principles," he said, "you represent the ignorant majority, and I the wise minority, decide that you are wrong and must yield."

> Thomas Fleming, *The Man Who Dared the Lightning* (1971), pp. 467–468, derived from "a collection of miscellaneous newspapers in the files of the American Philosophical Society" (p. 572). But the anecdote appears in Royall Tyler, *The Algerine Captive*

(1797), p. 181, where it is told concerning the satirist Dr. John Wolcot in a combat of wits with Tom Paine.

314.   "I [Harry Truman] always kept in mind something old Ben Franklin said at that meeting in Philadelphia we were talking about [the Constitutional Convention]. They had a big discussion about what should be done about ex-Presidents, and Alexander Hamilton I think it was said that it would be a terrible thing to degrade them by putting them back among the common people after they'd had all that power. But old Ben Franklin didn't agree. It's here someplace . . . I've got it, what he said. . . . ~~Here, read it.~~"

Franklin said, "In free governments the rulers are the servants and the people their superiors and sovereigns. For the former therefore to return among the latter is not to degrade them but to promote them."

Mr. Truman smiled, and he said, "I kept that in mind when I was in the White House, and I've had it in mind ever since I got my . . . promotion."

Merle Miller, *Plain Speaking, an Oral Biography of Harry S. Truman* (1974), pp. 431–432. Mr. Truman quoted from Franklin's debate with Gouvernor Morris (*Debates . . . Reported by James Madison*, ed. G. Hunt and J. B. Brown [1920], p. 325).

Appendix

Chronological
Index

Part 1:
In Franklin's
Own Writing

1730

1   Printers' errors turn the sacred to profane.

2   Jamaican curate the only one who hears voice from Heaven.

1731

3   Man and son bow to public opinion and drown ass.

1742

4   Poor Richard sees a signboard showing "Two Men at Law."

1751

5   Shoemaker disputes with wife on the value of time.

1753

6   Girl grows suddenly proud because of new silk garters.

7   Transylvanian Tartar observes that all men "love lazy."

8   Indian chief declines offer to school young braves.

1756

9   Maid, asked to air bedding, hangs it on hedge in midwinter.

1760

10   Lady, hearing dispute on Chinese shoe, asks if it *is* a shoe.

11   Cons a critic of Baskerville's types.

1762

12   Mayor rules those opposed to maypoles shall have none.

1764

13   Moor spares son's murderer because he has been a guest.

14   African chief protects white guest from vengeful mob.

1766

15 Tailors touring France mistake "Tout à l'heure."

1767

16 Frenchman accosts English travellers with a hot poker.

1768

17 Indians con missionary with fantastic fertility myth.
18 Cows are forbidden to suckle their calves.

1769

19 Sailor Jack is doing nothing and Tom is helping him.

1770

20 Eagle mistakes cat for rabbit.
21 Mastiff bullies lion cub till it grows larger.
22 Little boy fearing a whipping asked by another if he doesn't have a grand-
    mother.

1771

23 Vegetarian scruples overcome by frying cod.

1772

24 Forced to read edict for sports on Sunday, preacher adds the Fourth
    Commandment.
25 Rheumatism a worse *ism* than Arianism or Socinianism.

1773

26 Flies preserved in wine awake in a new world.
27 Weary sailor believes anchor cable has no end to it.
28 Cotton Mather warns to stoop.
29 "Edict of the King of Prussia" fools Paul Whitehead.
30 Sweep claims he is persecuted for wearing black.
31 Cook boils plum pudding without the bag.

(?) 1775

32 Montresor invited by St. Peter to sit where he pleases.

1778

33 Beggar rejects bishop's benediction as not worth twopence.
34 Guesses there must be a lot of good advice on the moon.
35 One servant cons another into carrying a harrow home alone.

1779

36 Buys a whistle for more than it is worth.

1782

37 Porter tells Peter the Great, "We're all czars here."
38 Angel says devils do not treat devils as men treat men.
39 Asked to referee an abusive argument, man tells adversaries they know
    each other.

1783

40 Debtor says his principles prevent his paying interest.
41 Indian chief declines offer to school young braves [variant of 8].
42 Indians con missionary with fantastic fertility myth [variant of 17].
43 Indian chief says church is where whites learn to cheat Indians.

1784

44 Black man observes that everyone works but the hog.
45 New homeowner puts "Omnia Vanitas" over doorway.
46 Declining duel, gentleman says adversary would stink worse.
47 Asking funds for college, James Blair told to make tobacco.
48 Cape May girls make worsted mittens to buy lace caps.
49 Wife buys him china bowl and silver spoon.
50 Blacksmith makes customer turn wheel to polish ax.

1785

51 Newgate prisoner loses buckles and complains of thieves.
52 Presbyterian onions flourish though damned.
53 Proud girl ultimately weds Irish Presbyterian parson.
54 Parisiennes are flat-chested from refusing to nurse.

1786

55 Betty the Chambermaid explains the spelling "y,f."

1787

56 Dr. Cooper says meat nearest the bone is sweeter.

1788

57 Story-teller makes queen and archbishop swear because that is his way of telling a story.
58 James Logan defends his un-Quakerlike militancy.
59 Moved by Whitefield's sermon, Hopkinson asks for a loan.
60 Whitefield told a favor is for his and not Christ's sake.
61 Sea captain orders his men to scour the anchor.
62 Chaplain Beatty serves run to increase attendance at prayers.

1789

63 Innis, the courier, says Loudon is like St. George.
64 William Shirley prefers a low seat to a high one.
65 Two-headed snake, undecided, dies of thirst.
66 Nothing can be said to be certain except death and taxes.

Part 2
In Writings
by Others

1777

82 Puns about glass being low in fallen barometer.
83 Claims it is Philadelphia that has taken Howe.

1778

84 Voltaire insists on speaking BF's language.
85 Lord Stormont will never warm himself at his stove.
86 British saw spirit of faction on his first embassy.
87 Confers with Galloway on independence.
88 Intended to meet his old master but never did.
89 Voltaire blesses his grandson.
90 Looking at Scone, he sees St. James's ruin.
91 Says spectators of Revolution do not pay.
92 Gallantry shows "mechanical rust" worn off.
93 On first day in Philadelphia, sleeps in a church.

1779

94 As young man, lived frugal life.

1783

95 Refuses to have anything to do with Mr. Z.
96 At Maidenhead, contrasts Thames with American rivers.
97 Tells Wedderburn he will make his master a little king.
98 Asked the use of balloons, asks the use of a newborn baby.
99 Refutes the maxim that all men are equally corrupt.
100 Wakened from nap by visitor (John Baynes).
101 Says America has no idle, thus no poor men.
102 Prints a peace pamphlet for a poor man.
103 Aristocrats cannot afford to marry on £40,000.
104 Robert Hunter Morris loved disputing.
105 Lewis Morris did not want a wife after he found one.
106 Elias Boudinot teased other children with a melon.
107 Anthony Morris overestimated Quaker antipathy to defense.
108 Quakers accepted "other grain" as synonym for gunpowder.
109 Anthony Morris, Sr., insisted reading was a waste of time.

1784

110 Abigail Adams dines with Mme Helvétius.

1785

111 Accused of wearing old coat to British treaty.
112 Insists on shaving himself in old age.
113 Had early intimations of revolution.
114 Believed tobacco would go out of fashion.
115 Interpreters, doctors, and debtors caused Turkish plagues.
116 Opposed slavery forty years.
117 Raynal says a voluble Frenchman is lost if he spits.

118 Warns against lending books.

119 Philosopher at the fair is happy in not wanting these things.

120 Next to their patients, quacks are greatest liars in the world.

121 Culprit says no one ever hanged a man worth 200,000 livres.

122 Mexican judges regret releasing peculator.

123 Cobbler turned postrider cures his consumption.

124 Says he could have bought independence at a tenth the cost of the war.

125 Says Latin and Greek are the quackery of literature.

126 Learned geography as a boy by gazing at maps during prayers.

127 Says Philadelphia has taken Howe [variant of 83].

128 Accused of wearing old coat to French treaty [variant of 111].

129 Sees himself as a remnant of old goods [variant of 80].

1786

130 Proposes wigmakers should form French army.

131 Visited by Winthrop Sargent.

132 King of Sweden refuses to meet him

1787

133 Mother says Plutarch gave him vegetarian notions.

134 Priestley says he cried at news of Boston Port Bill.

135 Priestley gave him religious books he never read.

136 Visited by Manasseh Cutler.

137 Says bicameral legislature is like two-headed snake [variant of 65].

138 Displays his library and inventions.

139 Recalls that the pope is infallible and the Church of England never wrong.

140 Recalls French lady insisting she knew no one but herself who was always right.

1788

141 Sets Raynal straight on authorship of "Polly Baker."

142 Tells British the Americans will settle for a few "re's."

143 Frenchman accosts English travellers with hot poker [variant of 16].

1789

144 Now certain the sun on back of Washington's chair is rising.

145 American in Paris jailed for sending him wine.

146 King of Prussia not wishing to ruin his trade refuses aid.

147 Washington recalls his saying stone walls have two sides.

148 Hopes to live long enough to intrude on posterity.

149 John Fitch incensed when he offers charity instead of support.

1790

150 Says a dying man can do nothing easy.

151 As a child, tells father to say grace once for all.

152 On deathbed, asks that "Life of Watts" be read to him.

153   George III insisted on using blunt lightning rods.

154   Expresses his pride in being a printer.

155   Toasts his old master, John Watts.

156   Tricking Keimer, he deletes "c" in "changed" [variant of *1*].

157   Tells a credulous man to believe what he sees.

158   Seeing spark ignite brandy, Indian says whites are clever.

159   Journeyman prefers to become gentleman by retail.

160   Warns legislators public can get along without them.

161   Blacksmith makes customer turn the wheel [variant of *50*].

162   Seeing luxuries manufactured at Norwich, asks what is manufactured for the factory workers.

163   Says he could have bought independence for one-quarter the cost of the war [variant of *124*].

164   Though he has not earned anything from the post office, neither has George III.

165   Not understanding French oratory, he applauds himself.

166   Shelburne said he had the "medicine expectative."

167   Watches two mistresses fight over him.

168   Says the French revolutionists served apprenticeship.

1791

169   Voltaire blesses his grandson [variant of *89*].

170   Jefferson says no one can "replace" him.

171   Frenchman offers to be king of America.

172   Rebuffs religious fanatic whose prophecy is too late.

173   Tells willing lass to wait till nights are longer.

1792

174   Wished to have a rational religious ritual.

175   Thought revolution impossible in 1766.

1795

176   Tries to electrocute turkey but electrocutes goose.

1796

177   Praises Frenchwomen of a certain age.

1797

178   Gibbon declines to meet him.

179   Lends freely to profligate cousin but refuses note.

180   Gives child three apples to show why rich are always tense.

1798

181   Wigmaker says his head is too big for wigs.

1800

182   His wife refuses repayment of loan she knew nothing about.

183   Preferred to get along with just one servant.

184   Visits house with small rooms and large columns.

1811

219 Carpenter shows him how to cut short a public statement.

220 Says youth good at making excuses is good for nothing else [variant of 206].

221 Fisherman tells him he has had a glorious nibble.

222 Quartermaster refuses to pay his commission.

1813

223 Tells of "rational man" who'd rather experiment than eat.

1815

224 When a boy, wished for one more beautitude.

225 His experiments electrify Philadelphia.

226 Assures guests his house is safest place in thunderstorm.

227 Composes an epigram for Miss Gunn.

1817

228 Scorned for mispronouncing "Cholmondeley," asks how the British pronounce "Cunningham."

229 Peale surprises him with a maid on his lap.

230 Sailor argues with him on nature of electricity.

?1818

231 Child asks mother if he is Brutus.

232 Says wearing spectacles keeps his eyes from being damned.

1818

233 Visits old printshop in London and toasts printing.

234 Says Anglican prayers did not bring king wisdom.

235 Points out that excluding mechanics from society would exclude God, "the greatest mechanic."

236 At chess, leaves king in check because expendable.

237 Aunt Franklin switches pack of cards for priest's commission.

238 Spartan's "sauce" is appetite from working hard.

239 Most pitiable is lonely man on rainy day who doesn't know how to read.

240 Fishing blacksmith uses a silver hook.

241 Wears blue-yarn stockings to French court.

242 Nurse says he looked at Christ's picture as he died.

243 Maintained it was Philadelphia that took Howe [variant of 83 and 127].

244 Dr. Pringle asks if old women are considered doctors.

245 Jonah swallows the whale [variant of 77].

246 Putting king in check, he takes it "as we do in America."

247 Emperor Joseph II says he is a king by trade.

248 Thompson the Hatter has his sign "amended."

249 Raynal's theory of American degeneracy disproven.

250 Raynal set straight on the authorship of "Polly Baker" [variant of 141].

?1818

251   Little girl complains of brother's eating on her side of bowl.

252   Man lacking sense of smell calls it pure fancy.

253   Cure for indigestion enables man to indulge freely.

254   Using opium, he gives up part of life for present ease.

255   Dr. Fothergill asks if old women are considered doctors [variant of 244].

1821

256   In old age, watches the passing scene impassively.

257   Feels in the way of new generation.

258   Envies fly released from corked bottle [variant of 26].

259   Uses hocus-pocus to calm the waves.

260   Moved to tears by Scotch song in the Alleghenies.

261   Lighthouse keepers quarrel and do not speak all winter.

262   Continues moving after king is taken at chess.

1823

263   As child, asks father to say grace once for all [variant of 151].

264   Fertilizes field to spell, "This field has been plastered."

265   French beauties crown him with laurels and kisses.

266   Refuses to force a tip on British tar.

1825

267   His mother says his vegetarian notions came from "some fool of a philosopher" [variant of 133].

268   Says villains would choose virtue if they knew its benefits.

269   Lived by *Proverbs* 3:16–17.

270   Fooled politicians by speaking the truth.

271   David Hume tells him America would manufacture men.

1826

272   Receives news of Burgoyne's defeat.

273   Assumes "Le digne Franklin" refers to Lee, Dean, and Franklin.

1827

274   Certain sun on back of Washington's chair is rising [variation of 144].

275   Sailor asks him if he invented sawdust pudding.

276   Would rather live on sawdust pudding than give up independence of a printer [variant of 216].

1828

277   Argues that suffrage should be based on man rather than ass.

278   Worries about companions' safety on Canada trip.

279   Vergennes tells him not to question accuracy of grant.

280   Asks if Samuel Chase still talks of girls and oysters.

281   On deathbed, cannot sit with old friend but can see him.

282   Izard called him "d——d old rascal" even posthumously.

1830

283 Serves sawdust pudding to show his independence [variant of 216 and 276].

284 Discovers that house is haunted by aeolian harp.

285 Adam Smith submitted *Wealth of Nations* for his correction.

286 Tells governor how to remember the name "Tocarededhogan."

287 Girl warned that he bottles lightning and thunder.

288 Tells Myers Fisher how to keep neighbors from tapping beer.

1834

289 West Indian innkeeper sends wife instead of wench into storm.

290 Urges Continental Congress to hang together or hang separately.

1840

291 Advises grandchildren to speak half as much as they hear or see.

1848

292 With giant Indian, intimidates Louis XVI.

1849

293 Advises youth to follow Scriptures in self-interest.

1850

294 Kind to young printer who follows advice on lightning.

?1853

295 New horse takes him to home of former owner's friend.

1854

296 Keeps raising price of book as customer haggles.

1858

297 Helps Benjamin West elope.

1859

298 Plays chess all night, sends for candles at dawn.

1861

299 Hopes new hospital will do more good than expected.

1864

300 Uses back door of his new house to avoid litigation.

301 Asks boys to play without so much noise.

302 Shows boy how to snuff a candle.

303 Bootblack tells him if everyone were frugal none would black shoes.

1869

304 Tries to electrocute a duck [variant of 176].

1881

305 Zabdiel Boylston aids him in London.

1887

306 Points out that lightning still strikes our nose and beard.

1898

307 Toasts Washington as Joshua [variant of *212*].
308 St. Peter admits Presbyterian as "a Christian."

1901

309 Rhode Island maiden repulses his advances.

1922

310 Tells old lady we have a republic if we can keep it.

1929

311 Confesses he loves best the girl who is nearest.

1965

312 Hosts Bailly in silence.

1971

313 A wise minority of one vanquishes aristocrats.

1974

314 Says a retiring president is being promoted.

Appendix

B

Index of
Reporters &
Repositories

Index of
Reporters &
Repositories

References Are to Anecdotes

185

American Magazine of Wit (1808), compiled by a New York Journeyman writer, Donald Fraser. Intended as an annual jestbook, it had at least 2,000 subscribers but appeared only once. *211-212*

American Museum, or, Universal Magazine (1787–1792) was founded by Mathew Carey in Philadelphia to reprint ephemeral literature that had appeared during the Revolution and thus establish the foundation of a truly national literature. *143, 146, 151, 153, 156, 173*

Arvine, Kazlitt (1819–1851), whose original name was Silas Wheelock Palmer, published a collection of 3,000 devout anecdotes in New York, 1849. *293*

Austin, Jonathan Loring (1748–1826), secretary of the Massachusetts Board of War, carried news of Burgoyne's surrender to BF and later became a successful merchant active in Federalist politics. *140-141*

Bancroft, Edward (1744–1821) served as BF's secretary in France and also edited his *Political and Miscellaneous Papers*, published in London, 1787. *204n*

Barbeu-du Bourg, Jacques (1709–1779) edited BF's scientific work in French, met him in 1767, and thereafter kept up a constant correspondence. *26*

Baynes, John (1759–1787), promising young lawyer, died soon after returning to England from a tour that included several visits to BF at Passy. *99-103*

Bent, Samuel Arthur (1841–1912), historian and journalist for the *New York Evening Post*, compiled his anecdotes in 1882–1887 as *Familiar Short Sayings of Famous Men*. *306*

Boston Magazine (1783–1786) had its best year in 1784, featuring original American essays, but then declined, imitating English magazines. *132*

Boylston, Nicholas Ward (1749–1828), successful merchant and philanthropist, he maintained homes in London and Princeton, Massachusetts, even during the Revolution. *305*

Buckingham, Joseph T. (1779–1861), in writing the history of early nineteenth-century journalism, gave us the biography of Benjamin Russell (1761–1845) who edited the *Massachusetts Centinel*. *294*

Burnaby, Andrew (1734?–1812), English traveler, kept copious notes on his tour of Virginia and New England, 1759–1760. *72*

Cabanis, Pierre (1757–1808) lived in Mme Helvétius's home during BF's visits but, alas, moralized his anecdotes. *267-270*

Callender, Hannah (1737–1801), Philadelphia Quakeress, kept a detailed diary from 1758 to 1762 when she married. *71*

Campan, Jeanne Louise Henriette (1752–1822), companion to Marie Antoinette, romanticized her memoirs. *265*

Carr, Robert (1776–1866) supplied the *Historical Magazine* with reminiscences of his boyhood as neighbor of BF. *300-303*

Carroll of Carrollton, Charles. See Gilmor, Robert.

The Casket, and Philadelphia Monthly Magazine (1826–1840), sometimes called "Atkinson's Casket," was a popular periodical. *275-277*

Chaplet of Comus (1811), published at Boston, was the last of the large-scale American jestbooks. *220-221*

Chaptal, John Anthony (1756–1832), or Jean Antoine, Comte Chaptal de Chanteloup, wrote widely used chemistry texts. *264*

Chaumont, Vincent le Ray de (1790–1866), grandson of le Ray de Chaumont, BF's landlord at Passy, compiled family anecdotes. *166*

Cobbett, William (1763–1835), political journalist, fled to England from Philadelphia to avoid libel suits and there reprinted his "Peter Porcupine" articles. *178*

Condorcet, Marie Jean (1743–1794), an aristocrat, early became a theorist of democratic liberalism, an activist in the French Revolution. *130, 169*

Coomb, Thomas, Jr. (1747–1822), son of an old friend of BF's, went to England in 1768 to be ordained and stayed there till 1772. *75-76*

Duane, William (1808–1882), son of Jackson's Secretary of the Treasury and great-grandson of BF, he edited family letters and the *Autobiography*, with a preface defending his great-grandfather from detractors. *291*

Ellicott, Andrew (1754–1820), surveyed the Mason-Dixon line before moving to Philadelphia where BF helped him obtain government assignments. *112*

L'Espion Anglais, ou Correspondance Secrète entre Milord All'Eye et Milord All'Ear (1777–1785), edited by M. Mairobert, was a periodical in epistolary form on gossip, politics, and literature. *83*

European Magazine (1782–1825) emphasized literature and fine arts, with profuse illustrations; published in London. *97*

Fanning, Nathaniel (1755–1805), native of Connecticut, was John Paul Jones's private secretary, then joined the French fleet when Jones's behavior became intolerable. *210*

Farrand, Max (1869–1945), distinguished historian of the Constitutional Convention and later the first director of the Huntington Library, edited the *Autobiography of BF*. *310*

Faÿ, Bernard (1893–1942), French scholar working with 600 unpublished letters in Paris archives, exploited BF's reputation as a lover of the ladies. *311*

Feast of Merriment; a New American Jester (1795), issued in New Jersey, derived chiefly from English jestbook, contained a few native jests. *176*

Federal Gazette and Pennsylvania Evening Post (1790–1793) was later called *Philadelphia Gazette and Commercial Intelligencer*. *172*

Fisher, Daniel (fl. 1755), English immigrant to Virginia, came with no success to Pennsylvania seeking a position, so BF employed him as a clerk till he could return to Virginia. *70*

Fitch, John (1743–1798), inventor of a steamboat, considered BF a rival for promoting competitor Daniel Bernouilli's ideas. *149*

Fleming, Thomas (1927–), among the leading professional biographers, incorporates anecdotes in lively narrative. *312*

Foote, Sam (1720–1777), most popular comedian of the eighteenth century, a hero of English jestbooks; could have met BF but they traveled in different circles. *206-209*

Ford, Paul Leicester (1865–1902), bibliographer of BF, was the great-grandson of Noah Webster and, despite physical handicap, produced much scholarship and several novels till killed by a brother in a dispute over money. *308*

Franklin, William Temple (1760–1823), illegitimate son of BF's son (who refused to recognize the boy for years); became his grandfather's private secretary and literary executor. *233-236*

Frankliniana (?1818), a Parisian jestbook compiled from BF's writings and other printed sources. *231-232*

French Louse, History of a (1779), attributed to a M Delauney, this foolish novel was translated in London the same year. *94*

Gazette of the United States (1789–1847), leading Federalist weekly, appeared the first year in New York and thereafter in Philadelphia, *146, 168*

Gentleman's Magazine (1731–1907), style-setting London monthly, set the mode for miscellany magazines, included among its proprietors David Henry (1710–1792), who had been a journeyman printer with BF in early life and remained one of his most ardent supporters and promoters. *84-85, 154-155*

Gilmor, Robert (1774–1848), prominent Bostonian bon vivant, was also an avid autograph collector. *278-283*

Glenbervie, Sylvester Douglas, Lord (1743 or 4–1823), wed to Lord North's eldest daughter, held various high posts in Parliament, and kept detailed diaries, 1793–1819. *194-197*

Grimm, Friedrich-Melchior, von (1723–1807), sent periodical reports to German princes from Paris where he was ambassador, 1753–1789. *91, 98*

Hewson, Mary (1739–1795), better known as Polly Stevenson, daughter of BF's London landlady, emigrated to America at his urging. *152*

Historical Magazine (1857–1876), a Boston monthly for history buffs, featured notes and queries. *299, 303*

Home Magazine (1852–1898), sometimes called "Arthur's," was edited in Philadelphia by T. S. Arthur, better known as author of "Ten Nights in a Barroom." *296*

Paine, Thomas (1737–1809), emigrated to Philadelphia in 1774 with testimonial from BF, became editor of the new *Pennsylvania Magazine*. *171*

Peale, Charles Willson (1741–1827), studied under Benjamin West in London, 1767–1769, before moving to Philadelphia in 1776. *229*

Percy Anecdotes (1820–1852), appeared first as a monthly periodical of anecdotes on specific themes-of-the-month, grew to 20 volumes by 1835. *289*

Pierce, William Leigh (c. 1740–1789), delegate from Georgia, wrote sketches of fifty-three of the fifty-five delegates to the Constitutional Convention. *148*

Priestley, Joseph (1733–1804), met BF in 1766 when, as a schoolmaster, he came to him to learn about electricity. *74, 134-135, 204*

Public Advertiser (1732–1794), among London's most respected dailies, featured foreign news as well as literature. *111*

Rush, Benjamin (1746–1813), native Pennsylvanian, studied medicine at Edinburgh and London, 1766–1768, became BF's lifelong friend. *79-80, 113-129, 150, 182, 205, 217, 222*

Sanderson, John (1783–1844), schoolmaster and writer of Philadelphia, compiled with his brother Joseph and others 7 volumes of biographies celebrating the signers of the Declaration of Independence. *266*

Sargent, Winthrop (1753–1820), a major in the Revolution, was in 1787 named acting governor of the Northwest Territory. *131*

Scots Magazine (1739), imitated the *Gentleman's Magazine*, trying to keep Scottish readers informed of European affairs. *96*

Seward, William (1747–1799) contributed anecdotes to the *European Magazine* totaling 5 volumes by 1797, two more by 1799. *177*

Silliman, Benjamin (1779–1864), Yale's first chemistry professor, had a long career popularizing science. *193, 295*

Smith, Margaret Bayard (1778–1844), wife of Jefferson's publicist, herself wrote novels and articles about Washington society. *213*

Thomas, Isaiah (1749–1831), Boston printer, moved his *Massachusetts Spy* to Worcester in 1775, later wrote history of Printing in America. *216*

Truman, Harry S. (1884–1972), said that BF's *Autobiography* taught him how to use time and to understand people. *314*

Tudor, William (1779–1830), a founder of the Boston *Athenaeum*, also founded the *North American Review*. *263*

Tyler, Royall (1757–1826), unsuccessful suitor for the hand of John Adams' daughter, became a lawyer and author of the first American comedy professionally produced (1787), *179-180, 228*

Vaughan, Benjamin (1751–1835), one of BF's closest friends in his old age,

Appendix

Index of
Subjects

Index of
Subjects

References Are to Anecdote Numbers

Designer:	Serena Sharp
Compositor:	Freedmen's Organization
Printer:	Vail-Ballou
Binder:	Vail-Ballou
Text:	Goudy
Cloth:	Joanna Arrestox B 44000
Paper:	50 lb. Smooth Cream